Miss Terry's Kitchen

By Terry Russell

Terry Russell
1400 Colorado Street C-16
Boulder City, NV 89005
E-mail TravelinTerry@gypsyjournal.net

Table Of Contents

Breakfasts

<u>Cakes & Sweet Treats</u>

Chicken

Cookies & Bars

Dips

Fish & Seafood

Main Dishes & Casseroles

Meats

Mexican Dishes

Miscellaneous

Pasta Dishes

Pies

Pizza

Salads

Soups & Stews

Vegetables & Sides

INTRODUCTION

I am an old fashioned cook. I cook from scratch, mostly without even thinking, and have been writing a cooking column in our Gypsy Journal RV Travel Newspaper for years. I love to cook and bake and while I enjoy eating out, it can become quite expensive. Dare I mention that I also LOVE food!!? I enjoy trying to duplicate specialty dishes that I have tasted in restaurants all over the country and I try to take advantage of the wonderful produce in farmer's markets, great meat in the local butcher shops, and the fresh seafood we encounter as we travel the highways and byways of this beautiful country of ours. I want to keep it fresh and interesting and to enjoy the natural flavors!

Over the years many of our readers have requested that I produce a cookbook with some of the recipes that my husband Nick always talks about in our travel newspaper and in his daily blog at www.gypsyjournalblog.com.
I even managed to put a couple of the most requested recipes up on a web page at http://gypsyjournalrv.com/category/miss-terrys-kitchen/ but somehow when we are traveling or when I get to weaving or crocheting or spinning, I don't get back to put up a new one. I promise to try and do better at updating it on occasion, if you promise to request recipes you would like to see at travelinterry@gypsyjournal.net

Though there are several recipes in this book that have been contributed to the recipe column in our newspaper, for which I give credit to the contributors, most are either everyday recipes or my versions of preparing certain dishes that I like or have grown up with. I throw in a few hints or suggestions along the way and occasionally attribute my husband's dislikes or allergies to a version of a recipe that has been changed to suit his needs. You will find simple hints and recipes for steaming vegetables and quickly sautéing meats all the way up to recipes for creating complicated breads and pies in this cookbook. May you enjoy your cooking adventure as much as I do!

DEDICATION

I wish to dedicate this cookbook to all of our readers, subscribers, and friends, but most especially I would like to dedicate to and to thank my husband and best friend in the world, Nick Russell, for all the ways that he contributes to and supports any effort of mine, in life and all of the things that I enjoy doing, like cooking and baking, weaving and other fiber arts, without ever complaining or fussing that I should be doing something else, other than this cookbook!! He has pushed and prodded, though gently for the most part, until I finally managed to accomplish what he knew I could. Thank you, my darling!

I also wish to thank my mother Bess Weber for standing me up in that chair and handing me a rolling pin all those years ago to roll out the crust on that first blueberry pie. Of course I have to thank my father, Pete Weber, for so thoroughly enjoying every dish ever created by his wife and daughters for all these years! My family has encouraged me and shared in my joy in cooking and baking as it has grown over the years. Thank you!

A big thank you to the many readers who submitted your recipes over the years. Many of them are included in this book. And a special thank you to Thelma Kitzmiller-Middleton, who custom made the beautiful apron I am wearing on the book's cover.

<u>TERRY'S TIPS</u>
(TOYS, TEMPS, TOOLS & OTHER THINGS)

The hardest part of cooking in an RV is adjusting to the limitations of an RV kitchen. I really miss the apartment-sized, extremely efficient stove that I built into the bus conversion we built and traveled in for years. Though I love our current motorhome, a Winnebago Ultimate Advantage, being restricted to three burners and a convection oven without a browning element was tying my hands!

I have found a couple of "tools" that have made my job a little easier. Though some convection ovens in RVs do have a browning or broiling element, several, including mine, do not. All of the items here can be found at most department stores and also can be purchased and shipped directly to your campground within two days from Amazon Prime. I bought a countertop Breville (Model BOV800XL A/ 120V) 1800-watt convection/toaster oven (currently priced at $249) that is capable of most of my requirements, including being able to fit a circular 13" pizza pan. (A cutting board top, pizza pan, and pizza baking stone are also available for this oven.) It heats up to 450° and bakes, roasts, toasts, and broils equally well! It is small enough to fit on my counter top and large enough to bake two full sized loaves of bread at the same time or a roast large enough to feed six or eight!

I have also added a 10" diameter Lodge Logic cast iron Dutch oven (currently priced at $35-50) to my pots and pans collection. It helps me to roast a whole chicken or a pork loin or eye round roast in the Breville oven to perfection, in just over an hour, with wondrous pan juices to create flavorful gravies or soup broths, and is also perfect for stovetop frying crisp and juicy chicken!

The third important item that I have found that I don't want to be without is an instant read thermometer (approximately $8-12). It helps me to be sure an item has cooked to a safe temperature or is done to perfection! I still use my built-in convection oven for larger or overflow items, but now have the smaller, more efficient oven for daily cooking and baking. The Dutch oven is great for both oven and stovetop cooking, and the instant read thermometer is my constant companion. Temperatures can be important, especially as you adapt to different cooking methods.

Most breads and rolls are done at 195° to 205°.
Chicken- 165°
Pork – Medium - 145° - Well done - 165°
Beef - Rare – 125° – 130° – Medium – 135° – 145° – Well 165°

Most propane RV ovens cook very hot from the bottom. I have found that using a small round pizza stone, placed directly on the floor of the oven, most definitely helps to moderate the temperature in the oven and keeps it from burning the bottoms of your baked items. The round stone lets the heat remain constant and allows the flame to breathe and burn evenly. Leave the baking rack in the normal baking position. Preheat your oven for an additional 15 to 20 minutes before baking. I left my stone in place all of the time and though it did eventually crack in half, either from heat or bouncing around, it still worked well for the entire time we had our first motorhome.

Some other simple items that I can't be without are:
- Dollar store clear plastic shower caps - perfect to cover bread rising in a bowl
- 2 small plastic cutting boards - one for meats and one for vegetables
- Good knives: The perfect general purpose/paring knife (mine fits my hand perfectly and can be used for almost everything; peeling, slicing, dicing etc.), a Yoshi blade ceramic knife (purchased for less than $20, plus it came with a ceramic vegetable peeler!), and a serrated bread knife
- Flat, flexible spreader (for butter, mayo, etc. usually available in threes)
- Flexible roll-up plastic dough mat for pastry and bread dough
- Nesting stainless steel mixing bowls, small, medium, and large
- Small food processor
- Coffee grinder (can be used for herbs and spices, too)
- An induction cooking plate for when you need an extra burner or if you want to cook outside using a large pot for boiling or frying that is too tall to use safely inside (for steaming that crab or lobster you got up in the northeast or northwest, or frying that chicken or fish that will stink up your rig for days!! (Cast iron works great on an

induction cook plate!)
- Several measuring cups and bowls, from a ¼ C measure all the way up to a 2-quart bowl, for both measuring and mixing in.

STANDARD WEIGHTS AND MEASURES

1 tablespoon = 3 teaspoons
2 tablespoons = 1 ounce
¼ cup = 4 tablespoons
1/3 cup = 5 1/3 tablespoons
½ cup = 8 tablespoons
1 cup = 8 ounces = 16 tablespoons
½ pint = 1 cup = 8 fluid ounces
1 pint = 2 cups = 16 fluid ounces
1 pound = 16 ounces
1 quart = 2 pints = 4 cups = 32 fluid ounces
1 gallon = 8 pints = 16 cups = 4 quarts = 64 fluid ounces

DRY WEIGHTS

½ ounce = 1 tablespoon = 15 g
1 ounce = 2 tablespoons = 30 g
4 ounces = ¼ pound = 120 g
8 ounces = ½ pound=225 g
12 ounces = ¾ pound = 360 g
16 ounces = 1 pound = 450 g

1 cup flour = 4 ounces = 150 g
1 cup sugar = 8 ounces = 225 g
1 cup butter = 2 sticks = 8 ounces = 225 g

STANDARD SUBSTITUTIONS

1 cup cake flour = 1 cup less 2 tablespoons of all purpose flour, plus 2 tablespoons cornstarch, whisked or sifted together to fluff

1 cup self-rising flour = 1 cup all purpose flour, less 2 teaspoons, plus 1 ½ teaspoons baking powder + ½ teaspoon salt

1 cup bread flour = 1 cup all purpose flour, less 1 teaspoon, plus 1 teaspoon wheat gluten

1 cup self-rising cornmeal = 1 cup cornmeal (either yellow or white) less 2 teaspoons plus 1 ½ teaspoon baking powder + ½ teaspoon salt

1 cup brown sugar = 1 cup white sugar mixed with 3 tablespoons molasses

1 cup powdered sugar = add 1 tablespoon cornstarch to a one cup measure and fill with white sugar. Process in a food processor until very fine and powdered

1 cup graham cracker crumbs = 13 to 15 squares of graham crackers

1 egg = 1 tablespoon ground flax seeds or chia seeds in 3 – 4 tablespoons warm water and left to soak for 5 minutes, or 3 tablespoons of mayonnaise, or enough mashed banana to measure ¼ cup, or ¼ cup of liquid egg substitute

Sweetened condensed milk = 1 cup plus 2 tablespoons nonfat dry milk powder, ½ cup warm water, ¾ cup sugar. Place warm water in a bowl with dry milk powder. Mix well and add in sugar, mixing well.

Biscuit mix = 4 cups all purpose flour, ¾ cup dry milk powder, 1/3 cup baking powder, 1½ teaspoon salt and ¾ cup shortening. Whisk together dry ingredients and cut in shortening until crumbly. Store in an airtight container.

Seasoning salt = 1 cup salt, 1 teaspoon thyme, 1 ½ teaspoon garlic powder, 2 teaspoons onion powder, 2 teaspoons dry mustard powder, 2 teaspoons curry powder, 2 teaspoons paprika, 2 teaspoons turmeric, and 1 teaspoon sugar. Store in an airtight container.

GENERAL MEAT COOKING CHART (at 350^0)
PORK
Rib or loin, fresh, 4 – 8 pounds 30 – 40 minutes per pound
Picnic shoulder, bone-in, fresh or smoked, 5 – 10 pounds, 40 minutes per pound
Boned and rolled shoulder, fresh, 3 – 7 pounds, 60 minutes per pound
Ham, smoked, Under10 pounds, 20 minutes per pound – 12 – 20 pounds, 18 minutes per pound

BEEF
Rolled and boned roasts
For rare, 3 – 8 pounds, 40 minutes per pound plus 15 minute resting time
For medium, 3 – 8 pounds, 45 minutes per pound plus 15 minute resting time
For well done, 3 – 8 pounds, 55 minutes per pound plus 15 minute resting time

POULTRY
Chicken, 3 – 5 pounds, 40 minutes per pound, 5 – 7 pounds, 35 minutes per pound
Turkey, 8 – 10 pounds 20 minutes per pound, 18- 20 pounds – 14 minutes per pound

OVEN TEMPERATURES

Slow = 250^0 - 300^0
Moderate = slow - 325^0, medium - 350^0, quick - 375^0, hot - 400^0
Hot = 425^0 to 450^0
Extremely Hot = 475^0 - 500^0

MY STAPLE PANTRY ITEMS

You need to determine your own specific needs. This is just an outline and may be much more or less than you require. We live and travel in a motorhome fulltime and I prefer fresh or frozen fruits and vegetables and will shop more frequently for these items so I don't stock many canned items. I cook from scratch and frequently bake bread and pizza and like to include healthy ingredients so I carry many more dry pantry items and flours than you might.

- All purpose flour
- Bread flour, optional
- High gluten, high protein flour, for pizza dough
- Semolina flour, for pizza baking
- White whole-wheat flour, for bread (keep in refrigerator)
- Wheat gluten or enhancer
- Baking cocoa
- Golden flax seeds (whole, to grind before using) keep in refrigerator

- Chia seeds
- Old-fashioned oats
- White sugar
- Dark brown sugar
- Turbinado (raw) sugar
- Honey
- Molasses
- Baking powder
- Baking soda
- Cornstarch
- Olive oil
- Vegetable oil
- Vinegar, white, cider, champagne, and Balsamic
- Worcestershire sauce
- Oyster sauce
- Fish sauce
- Tamari (soy) sauce
- Sriracha sauce
- Catsup/ketchup
- Regular and/or butter flavored shortening
- Regular table salt
- White long grain rice (dry)
- Jasmine rice (dry)
- Arborio rice (dry)
- Quinoa, red and black (dry)
- Pinto beans (dry)
- Black (turtle) beans (dry)
- Lentils and split peas (dry)
- Non-fat dry milk powder
- Tomato paste
- Diced tomatoes in juice
- Tomato puree
- Chicken broth
- Peanut butter
- Jam and/or jelly
- Tuna
- Flat anchovies in olive oil
- Angel hair pasta
- Penne pasta or macaroni

- Evaporated milk
- Sweetened condensed milk

MY "GO TO" SPICES AND HERBS

- Almond extract
- Basil leaves, dried
- Bay leaves, whole
- Caraway seeds
- Cardamom, ground
- Cayenne (red pepper)
- Celery seeds
- Celery salt
- Chili powder
- Chipotle powder
- Cilantro leaves, dried
- Cinnamon, ground (and stick, optional)
- Cloves, ground
- Cream of tartar
- Cumin, ground
- Dill weed, dried
- Fennel seeds
- Garlic powder
- Ginger, ground
- Lemon extract
- Marjoram leaves, dried
- Nutmeg, ground
- Onion powder
- Oregano leaves, dried
- Paprika, both sweet and smoked, ground
- Parsley leaves, dried
- Peppercorns for grinding; black and mixed (pink, white, green, etc.)
- Poppy seeds
- Red chili, crushed, dried
- Rosemary, crushed, dried
- Sage leaves, crushed, dried
- Sea salt (grinder)
- Smoked sea salt (grinder)
- Sesame seeds, raw

- Thyme leaves, dried
- Truffle oil or salt, optional
- White pepper, ground
- Vanilla, real extract and beans, optional

KITCHEN TOOLS

- Hand operated can opener
- Cheese slicer
- Hand grater
- Microplane (zester-grater)
- Garlic press
- Rolling pin
- 2 - 6-Cup cupcake pans
- 1 - 9" square baking pan
- 2 - 8" round cake pans
- 2 - 8" square baking pans
- 1 - 7x11" baking pan
- 1 - 9x13x2" baking pan
- 2 – pie pans
- 2 – 9x5" or 8x4" loaf pans
- 1 - 12" round pizza pan
- 1 pizza stone
- 1 deep casserole baking dish
- Roll of aluminum foil
- Roll of wax paper
- Roll of plastic wrap
- Roll of parchment paper
- Silicone baking spatula(s)

COOKING TOOLS

- 10" cast iron Dutch oven with lid
- 10" cast iron skillet
- 8" cast iron skillet
- 2 – 1-quart saucepots with lids
- 1 gallon-sized heavy soup or saucepan with lid
- 1 deep heavy pasta pot with lid
- 1 extra large (20") heavy skillet
- 1 double-boiler insert, optional

- 1 steamer insert, optional

APPETIZERS

ARTICHOKE AND SPINACH APPETIZER

2 - 8-oz. pkg. cream cheese, softened
½ C mayonnaise
4 T butter, softened
6 T milk
1 C grated Parmesan cheese
2 cloves garlic, minced
1/8 tsp cayenne pepper (or to taste)
2 – 14 oz. cans artichoke hearts, drained and chopped
2 – 10 oz. pkg. frozen chopped spinach, thawed and drained
Preheat oven to 350°. Mix all ingredients, except Parmesan, with electric mixer until fluffy. Place in lightly greased 3 qt. casserole. Sprinkle with Parmesan. Bake for 25 – 30 minutes until lightly browned. Serve with crackers, pita chips, tortilla chips, or vegetable strips. Submitted by Nancy Benjamin.

APPETIZER BEEF MEATBALLS

1 lb. lean ground beef
¾ C water
½ C vacuum packed toasted wheat germ
1/3 C soy sauce
1 tsp freshly grated ginger root (or ¼ tsp ground ginger)
1 clove garlic, minced
2 T catsup
Mix all ingredients together in a large bowl. Form into 6 dozen bite sized balls (or make into regular sized meatballs for a regular dinner entrée) and place in a single layer in a shallow baking pan. Bake small ones at 450⁰ for 6 – 8 minutes, or large ones for 18 – 20 minutes, until cooked as desired. There will be some sauce. Garnish with toasted sesame seeds and minced parsley and serve small ones with toothpicks, as appetizers.

RANCH PINWHEELS

2 - 8 oz. pkg. cream cheese, softened
1 - 4 oz. pkg. dry ranch dressing mix
¼ C minced bell peppers
¼ C celery, minced
¼ C green onions, minced
¼ C stuffed olives, chopped
¼ C cooked ham, minced or 1 small can of deviled ham (optional)
4 - 12" flour tortillas

In a bowl, mix cream cheese and dressing mix. When smooth, add all remaining ingredients except tortillas and mix well. Divide and spread evenly over tortillas and roll up tightly. Wrap tortillas in plastic and chill for two hours. To serve, cut into ½" slices.

DEVILED HAM SALAD SPREAD

1 – 8 oz. pkg. cream cheese, at room temperature
½ C mayonnaise
1 – 4.25 oz. can deviled ham
1 C diced celery
¼ C chopped green pepper
2 T chopped pimiento
1 T minced onion

Mix all together and chill for 30 minutes or more. Serve in crisp lettuce cups, as a dip for crackers, or as a sandwich spread on white bread with crisp lettuce. This was (and still is) a favorite of mine from childhood, a nice comfort food, mostly used as a sandwich spread, but great on wheat crackers, too!

CHEESE HERMITS

8 oz. sharp cheddar, grated
1 C (2 sticks) butter
½ tsp baking powder
2 C flour
¼ tsp salt
1 T Worcestershire sauce
Dash cayenne pepper

Melt butter in a large heavy saucepan. Remove from heat and stir in grated cheese, Worcestershire, and cayenne. In a separate bowl, combine flour, baking powder, and salt. Work into cheese mixture until well combined. Shape into small balls and bake at 350° on an ungreased baking sheet for 15 to 20 minutes, until deeply golden brown. Great to serve for happy hour!

FAVORITE SNACK MIX

2 - 10.5 oz. boxes cheese snack crackers
½ C vegetable oil
1 – 1 oz. pkg. Hidden Valley Ranch Dressing mix
1 heaping T dried dill
1 tsp garlic powder
1 tsp celery salt

Place the crackers in a large sealable freezer container or zip top bag. In a bowl, mix the oil, salad dressing mix, dill, garlic powder, and celery salt. Pour this mixture over the crackers, cover (or seal), and invert to coat the crackers with seasonings. Refrigerate for at least 24 hours, turning the container every so often to keep the crackers coated. Bring to room temperature to serve. Chill leftovers, if any. Submitted by Pat Dunkel.

SWEET AND SPICY POPCORN

3 T vegetable oil
½ C popcorn kernels
3 T sugar
2 T ancho chili powder
2 tsp salt

Heat oil and 3 popcorn kernels in a heavy pot with a lid, over medium high heat. When kernels pop, add sugar and remaining popcorn. Cover pot, and cook, shaking pot (while on burner) every 10-15 seconds, until the popping is down to one every 2-3 seconds. Remove from heat and stir in chili powder and salt. Submitted by Cleo Collette.

<u>BREADS</u>

QUICK BREAD
2 C whole-wheat flour
1 C unbleached flour
1 C sugar
2 tsp sea salt (or only 1 tsp of table salt)
2 tsp baking <u>soda</u>
2 C buttermilk
Preheat regular or convection oven to 375° and lightly grease or spray a loaf pan. In a large bowl, combine flours, sugar, and salt. In a smaller bowl, combine baking soda with buttermilk. It will begin to increase in size. Pour buttermilk mixture into the flour mixture and mix well. Pour into loaf pan and let rise until increased by 1/3 in size. Put loaf into the center of heated oven; decrease heat to 350° and bake for 1 hour. Turn out of pan after 5 minutes and cool slightly on rack. Slice and serve while warm.

SUNDAY DINNER ROLLS

1 (.25 ounce) package active dry yeast OR 2¼ tsp instant yeast
¼ C warm water
1 pinch white sugar
1/3 cup white sugar
2 eggs
1 C warm milk
½ C butter at room temperature
1 tsp salt
4 C all-purpose flour

In a measuring cup, stir yeast, ¼ C warm (110^0) water, and a pinch of sugar. In a large bowl, beat eggs with 1 C warm milk; add butter and salt. When yeast is foamy (5 – 10 minutes), mix yeast mixture into egg mixture and add sugar. Gradually stir in flour. Cover with a damp cloth and allow to stand at room temperature for 1 hour, then place in the refrigerator and allow to raise overnight. This dough is rather sticky and will rise to at least twice its size. Divide the dough into 4 equal portions. Roll each section out into a circle on a floured board or wax paper. Cut into pizza slice shapes and roll slices, large end to small end. Place on greased flat baking sheets and allow to raise for 2 hours. Bake at 375^0 for 8 minutes. Makes 32 rolls.

QUICK PECAN BREAD

2 cans (8 count) crescent rolls
2 T butter, softened
½ C sugar
2 tsp cinnamon
¼ C chopped pecans
Topping:
2 T butter, melted
¼ C powdered sugar
2 T honey
1 T vanilla

Grease a 9X5" loaf pan. Roll out each package of un-separated crescent rolls, separately, onto waxed paper. Spread each piece with softened butter. Mix sugar, cinnamon, and nuts together. Sprinkle this mixture over the butter. Roll dough, starting at long end, and place in loaf pan, 1 - 8 roll package as a bottom layer and the other on top. Bake at 350^0 for 30 – 35 minutes. Remove from pan while still hot and place top side up. Combine topping ingredients and drizzle over loaf. Serve warm.

TERRY'S OAT & FLAX BREAD

1 medium russet potato, peeled & diced
1-quart water
1 tsp white sugar
1 T bread flour
2 T instant (bread machine) yeast
2½ C old-fashioned oats
1/3 C freshly ground golden flax
2-3 T toasted wheat germ
2-3 T chia seeds
¼ C molasses
3 T turbinado or brown sugar
½ C butter, room temperature
1 1/3 C powdered milk
3½ – 4½ C unbleached bread flour
3 T bread dough enhancer (or vital wheat gluten)
1 T sea salt

1. In a large heat resistant bowl, measure out and add in 2½ cups of old fashioned, or rolled oats. I'm sure the quick cooking will also work here, but I prefer the regular rolled oats. Add up to ½ cup of additional healthy options, to include: ground golden flax, toasted wheat germ, chia seeds, and cooked black or red quinoa. I have used all flax, all red quinoa, and this batch, in which I placed 2 T toasted wheat germ and 2 T chia seeds into a ½ cup measure and finished filling it up with the ground golden flax. It was scrumptious! Now add in ½ C butter, cut into pieces, ¼ C molasses, and 3 T turbinado sugar (or increase the molasses). Set aside.

2. Peel and dice a medium russet potato and boil it in a quart of water. Cook until very tender, 15 – 20 minutes, and pour 2½ C of the boiling potato water over the oats in the bowl. Let set for 20 minutes or so.

3. Pour 1/3 C of the remaining potato water into a 1 C measure and let it cool to 110^0. Once the water has cooled, stir in 1 tsp white sugar and 1 T flour. Mix well, and stir in 2 T instant (bread machine) yeast. Set aside to get foamy for 10 minutes or so.

4. Finish draining the potatoes (reserve any remaining water) and mash very well. Stir them into the oat mixture, adding some of the reserved potato water to make a slightly loose mixture.

5. In the bowl of a bread mixer or a stand mixer set up with the bread hook, combine 3½ cups of unbleached bread flour, 1 1/3 cups of powdered milk,

3 T bread enhancer or vital wheat gluten, and 1 T sea salt.

6. Combine the yeast mixture and the oat mixture and pour it over the flour mixture. Turn the mixer on low and mix for 2 – 3 minutes, until well combined. If the mixture appears too wet, add in more bread flour, a tablespoon or two at a time, just until the dough no longer sticks and comes away on your finger when you touch it. You want a nice, soft, slightly wet dough, tacky, but not sticky. Now let the mixer knead the dough for 6 – 8 minutes to develop the gluten. If you don't have a mixer, knead by hand on a lightly floured surface for 10 – 12 minutes, trying not to add in any more flour than you have to, to keep it from sticking to your hands. After it is machine kneaded, you may wish to turn it out onto a lightly oiled surface, and with floured hands, gently shape into a ball. Either way, turn the dough ball into a large bowl that you have poured 2 T olive oil into, and turn to coat all sides. Cover and let rest until it doubles in size, about 1½ hours.

7. For machine kneaded, go to next step.

If hand kneaded, very gently deflate, by slowly pushing your fist into the dough ball and turning it over, tucking the sides underneath. Cover and let rise again, for about 30 minutes.

8. On a lightly oiled surface (a pastry and rolling mat works very well here), very gently dump the risen dough out and very gently flatten and shape into a rectangle, gently patting out any air bubbles. Divide into 4 even pieces, and tightly roll and shape into loaves, placing in oiled loaf pans. Cover and let rise until ¼ – ½" above the top edge of the pans. Preheat oven (convection oven, too) to 350°. I did three of these loaves in the convection oven in my RV, at one time, and put one loaf in my Breville Smart Oven. They all look the same, and taste the same, but the one in the Breville baked 4 or 5 minutes faster. Of course, it was by itself and that makes a difference. (I now do two loaves at a time in the Breville.)

9. If you have a clean spray bottle, lightly spray (mist) the tops of the loaves with water, and slash with a very sharp knife or razor blade, about ½" deep, JUST BEFORE placing loaves into the oven. (This will cause the loaf to spring into action and raise up very nicely as it starts baking.) Bake for 28 – 30 minutes, until well browned, and bread temperature reaches 190-205° on an instant read thermometer, or the loaf sounds hollow when thumped. After 5 minutes, turn loaves out of pans onto a cooling rack and if desired, brush the loaves lightly with butter for a softer crust. Cool completely before slicing. This bread has a nice clean slice and is wonderful for sandwiches and toast!

BATTER OATMEAL BREAD

¾ C boiling water
3 T butter or shortening
1 tsp salt
½ C quick oats
¼ C molasses or brown sugar
1 pkg. yeast, mixed into ¼ C warm water and set aside for 5 minutes, until foamy
2¾ C all purpose flour
1 egg, lightly beaten

In a large heatproof bowl, pour boiling water over the oats. Add butter, salt, and molasses and let stand until cool. Add remaining ingredients and mix well. Pour into a greased 9X5" loaf pan and let rise for 45 minutes. Bake at 350° for 45 minutes.

POTATO TOASTING BREAD

1 medium large russet potato, peeled and cubed to 1" pieces
1¼ C reserved potato water
2½ tsp instant yeast (aka bread machine yeast) OR 1 - .25 oz. pkg. active dry yeast
2 T sugar
2 T butter
½ tsp salt
¼ C dry instant milk powder
3½ - 4 C unbleached bread flour (King Arthur is my favorite).
Olive oil and/or non-stick spray for greasing bowl and (2) 4 ½ X 8 ½" loaf pans

This is a dense, yet moist and tender bread, with lots of flavor, perfect for morning toast and jam, along with your morning coffee. Nick has always chosen a potato bread from the grocery store for his bread preference, and I have frequently used potato water to proof my yeast, or potato flour or starch in with the flour for extra tenderness in a lot of my bread baking, so taking it a bit further was a natural stepping stone. For this bread, I use the whole potato, but I do peel the potato first. Place potato in a small saucepan and cover with water. Bring to a boil and cook for approximately 15 minutes, or until tender. Drain potato water into a heat resistant 2 cup measuring cup. Add enough water to measure 1¼ C. Set aside to cool to

110° degrees (cool enough that you can keep your finger in it). Add yeast and ½ tsp sugar to potato water when it has cooled and set aside until foamy. Mash potato until smooth with a fork, adding in 2 T butter and remaining sugar. In a large mixing bowl, combine 2 C of the flour, powdered milk and salt. Stir together yeast mixture and potato mixture and add to flour mixture. Combine with a wooden spoon, mixing until it all comes together. Add in 1 C flour and stir it in. At this point, I like to turn the dough out onto a floured rolling mat and begin kneading it, adding in enough of the remaining flour to come together into a smooth and elastic ball, tacky, but not sticky, kneading for about 8 – 10 minutes. It will be a soft dough. Place dough into a bowl greased with a tablespoon or two of olive oil, turning to grease all, lightly cover, and let raise until double, anywhere from 30 – 90 minutes, depending on temperature in your kitchen. When doubled, gently deflate and divide in half, gently rolling and shaping to fit into pans. Lightly cover with plastic wrap and let rise until ½ " taller than pan. Preheat your (convection or regular) oven to 375 °. When oven is ready, bake bread for 28 – 30 minutes until darkly golden brown. Turn out of pan onto a cooling rack and let cool for at least 20 minutes before any attempt is made to cut it. For a softer crust, lightly butter the tops of your bread. Cool completely before storing.

STAR QUALITY CHILI CORN BREAD

2½ C flour
2 C corn meal
¼ C sugar
8 tsp baking powder
1 tsp salt
½ tsp garlic powder
4 eggs, lightly beaten
1 2/3 C buttermilk
½ C butter at room temperature
1 – 15 oz. can creamed corn
2 – 4 oz. cans diced green chilies
1 C shredded sharp cheddar cheese

In a large mixing bowl, whisk together flour, corn meal, sugar, baking powder, salt, and garlic powder until fluffy. Whisk in eggs, buttermilk, and softened butter until combined. Stir in creamed corn, green chilies, and cheddar and pour into a non-stick sprayed 9X13X2" pan and bake in a preheated 375^{0} oven for 30 minutes, until golden brown and toothpick inserted in center of bread comes out clean or with cheese or crumbs clinging.

GRIDDLE FLAT BREAD

2 C all purpose flour
1 scant tsp salt
2 tsp baking powder
¼ tsp baking soda
3 T butter flavor shortening
2/3 C ice water

Combine dry ingredients in a medium mixing bowl. Cut in shortening with a fork until crumbly and well blended. Stir in ice water until it forms a ball. Turn out onto a floured surface and gently knead together into a ball. Divide into 5 equal pieces and roll each into a 1/8" thick circle approximately 6 - 8" in diameter. Prick dough with a fork and cook on a well oiled griddle heated to medium high heat. Turn with a spatula after 30 - 45 seconds, when brown spots have formed, and cook for another 30 - 45 seconds or until done. Watch closely as they cook fast. While still hot, top one half with a slice or two of Muenster or Provolone cheese and some thinly sliced deli roast beef or turkey and your favorite condiments and veggies (tomato, avocado, onion, etc.) fold to eat, and enjoy. PB & J is also a treat on this bread, or butter while still hot and top with cinnamon sugar or honey and cut into wedges to serve. Note* You can fry this bread in 1 T vegetable or olive oil for a crispier treat.

MY FAVORITE FLOUR TORTILLAS

2½ C all-purpose flour
1 tsp salt (use less or no salt if using bacon grease)
1 tsp baking powder
¼ C dry non-fat milk powder
½ C lard or cold bacon fat/lard combo (or use butter or shortening)
1½ - 2 C boiling water

Whisk the flour, salt, powdered milk, and baking powder together in a mixing bowl. Mix in the lard with your fingers until the flour resembles cornmeal. Add the boiling water and mix until the dough comes together; place on a lightly floured surface and carefully (when cool enough) knead a few minutes until smooth and elastic. Place back in bowl, covered, to rest for 30 minutes. Divide the dough into 8 equal pieces and roll each piece into a ball. Preheat a large cast iron skillet over medium-high heat for several minutes. Use a well-floured rolling pin on a lightly floured surface to roll a dough ball into a thin, round tortilla. Place onto the hot dry skillet, and cook until bubbles are browning, flattening dough as bubbles rise up; then flip and continue cooking until brown on the other side. Place the cooked tortilla on a clean dishtowel, folding towel to cover the tortilla, and continue rolling and cooking the remaining dough, stacking the cooked tortillas to steam inside the towel. Serve hot and buttered with cinnamon sugar, or in your favorite recipe for burritos or fajitas. When completely cooled, store in zip top plastic bag.

INDIAN FRY BREAD

2 C flour
1T baking powder
1½ tsp salt
¼ C shortening
½ C warm water
vegetable oil for frying

Whisk together flour, baking powder, and salt. Cut in shortening until mixture is the texture of cornmeal. Gradually add in up to ½ C warm water, adding only enough to make the dough come together. Knead dough on a lightly floured surface until soft and pliable. Roll into fist sized balls, cover and let rest for 10 minutes. Heat 1½" oil in a large heavy skillet over medium heat for at least 10 minutes. Pat out dough and flatten by hand into a pancake sized disc about ¼ " thick. Gently slip one disc at a time into hot oil and fry until golden brown on both sides, using a fork to turn. Drain on paper towels. Repeat with remaining dough balls. Serve with powdered sugar and honey or use for Indian tacos.

OVERNIGHT CINNAMON ROLLS

1 medium russet potato, peeled, cubed, and boiled until soft, reserve ¼ C cooking water
1 C milk (heated approximately 1 minute in microwave)
¼ C reserved warm potato water (110°.)
1 T pure vanilla
½ C butter (one stick), at room temperature
2 eggs, at room temperature, beaten
½ tsp salt
½ C plus 1 tsp granulated sugar
5 C unbleached bread flour
1 T vital wheat gluten
3 tsp instant yeast
Cinnamon Filling:
½ C butter, melted
1 C firmly-packed brown sugar
5 T ground cinnamon
1 tsp ground cardamom
¾ – 1 C raisins (optional)

1 T Granulated Sugar
Butter Frosting
Cream together:
2 oz. cream cheese, at room temperature
¼ C butter, melted and cooled
1 C powdered sugar
1 tsp pure vanilla
To simplify things, peel and cube a medium russet potato and boil, in enough water to cover, until tender, approximately 15 minutes. Drain ¼ C of the boiled potato water into a 1 C measuring cup and let it cool to 110 degrees (I can keep my finger in it). Discard any extra water. Once cooled enough, add three teaspoons instant yeast and 1 teaspoon sugar to reserved potato water and set it aside until it gets nice and foamy. In the same pot you boiled the potato, mash it up with a fork, adding in ½ C room temperature butter and ½ C sugar. Mash and mix this together until it is smooth. Heat 1 C of milk for 1 minute in the microwave on high, and add it to the mashed potato mixture, along with 1 tablespoon of pure vanilla. Beat 2 eggs with a fork (in the cup you warmed the milk–don't want too many dishes) and add it to the pot. By now your yeast should be nice and foamy, so pour it into the pot, too.

In a large mixing bowl, combine 3 cups of unbleached bread flour, 1 tablespoon of vital wheat gluten (if you have it) and ½ tsp of salt. If you have a stand mixer, now is the time to use it. Otherwise, use your big wooden spoon. Pour your liquid potato mixture over the flour mixture and combine to make a soft dough. Change to a dough hook and stir in remaining 2 cups unbleached flour. Let dough hook work at a medium low speed for 6 –8 minutes, or, if you are doing it by hand, once combined, turn out onto a lightly oiled surface and knead for 8 – 10 minutes. Try not to add in any additional flour or your bread may become tough. This will be a soft dough. Place dough into an oiled bowl, turning to coat dough with oil, cover with plastic or a dishtowel, and let rest for 15 minutes.

At this time I would like to explain a couple of things. Instant yeast does not have to be combined with a liquid to proof. It can be combined with the dry ingredients and then have warm liquids added to do its job, as in a bread machine. It does, however improve its efforts when it is combined with a liquid and a bit of sugar to give it a kick start. There are a couple of things that yeast doesn't like. Milk enzymes and salt. That is why we heat the milk first; to decrease the enzyme action. And, we keep the salt away until the yeast has activated. Oh, and have I mentioned dollar store shower caps? For a buck you can get 15 clear plastic elasticized (disposable) shower caps to cover your mixing bowls and other containers for short term, like resting or rising bread. (-: Gently place your dough onto a lightly oiled surface and flatten and shape into an approximately 15" X 24" rectangle. If it doesn't cooperate, let it rest for 5 or 10 minutes while you melt ½ C of butter and mix in 1 C packed, brown sugar, 5 tablespoons of a good ground cinnamon, and a tsp of ground cardamom for the filling. Gently finish shaping the dough.

Now, sprinkle and spread the brown sugar mixture, as evenly as you can, over the dough, using your fingers, the spatula, or the back of a spoon. If you want to add in nuts and raisins, now is the time. I like to scatter about 3/4 cup of each over the dough, then top with about a tablespoon of granulated sugar before I roll up the dough, forming a nice fat log. Tug or pull to keep things kind of even. Don't worry about how it looks right now. Once it's baked, no one will notice!

Okay, now you can cut it into 12 pieces, using a serrated knife, or....... dental floss!!! The floss makes a nice, clean cut. Slide an 18" piece under the log to the very center. Cross the ends over each other on the top, and pull in opposite directions and you can get a clean cut. Repeat, and you get the job done fairly easily, once you get the hang of it. To help get even pieces, cut into 2 equal pieces, then divide those pieces in half, and each half then into thirds and you will get 12 pieces. Butter a 9X13X2" baking pan and place the rolls in the pan, gently pressing them to level them. Lightly spray with non-stick spray and cover with plastic wrap. You can place in the refrigerator to rise slowly overnight, or you can let rise for 45 minutes to an hour and bake.

In the morning, set out for a half hour to an hour to come to room temperature and raise a bit, then lightly spritz with water (it gives the bread an extra lift to rise) and bake at 365° for 30 –35 minutes, to an internal temperature of 190-205° on an instant read thermometer. Once done, set on a cooling rack, or your stovetop, and mix your frosting up while you wait for them to cool a bit, then slather frosting generously over and serve while warm. If you have any left, wrap in foil. To reheat, place foil packet in the oven for 4 or 5 minutes, or cover with a paper towel and microwave on high, on a paper plate, one at a time, for 45-60 seconds.

ANGEL BISCUITS

1 (.25 ounce) package active dry yeast or 2¼ tsp instant (bread machine) yeast
¼ C warm water (about 110°)
½ tsp sugar, agave syrup, or honey
2 C warmed buttermilk (about 110°)
5 to 5¼ C all-purpose flour
¼ C granulated sugar
2 tsp baking powder
1 tsp baking soda
1 T salt
1 C chilled butter (2 sticks)
melted butter (optional, for topping)

Dissolve the yeast in the ¼ C of warm water with ½ tsp of your sweetener of choice. Set aside. In a large mixing bowl combine flour, sugar, baking powder, baking soda, and salt. Cut in cold butter until mixture resembles coarse meal, with some small pea-size pieces of butter. Stir in yeast mixture and buttermilk, blending well. Turn dough out onto a lightly floured surface and knead with floured hands just a few turns and pat into a round about ½ inch thick. Cut with 2 to 2½ inch biscuit cutters. Place cut out biscuits on a lightly greased baking sheet. Cover with a dishtowel and let rise in a warm place for about 30 minutes. Bake at 400° for about 15 to 20 minutes. Brush tops with the melted butter while still hot. Makes about 2 to 3 dozen angel biscuits, depending on size. This recipe can be easily halved, but use ¼ C warm water and ½ tsp sweetener of choice with 1¼ tsp yeast, halving the remaining ingredients.

BUTTERMILK BISCUITS

2 C flour
2 tsp baking powder
1 tsp baking soda
¼ C butter, cut into small cubes
½ tsp salt
2/3-3/4 C buttermilk

Sift flour, salt, baking soda, and baking powder together. Add butter, cutting in with a fork. Add just enough buttermilk to make a soft dough. Gently knead and pat into a 1/3" thick rectangle. Cut into 2 - 2½" circles and place on ungreased baking sheet and bake at 400° for 10 - 12 minutes until golden brown. (For cheddar/herb biscuits, substitute 1 tsp garlic salt for regular salt and add ½ C shredded cheddar when you cut in butter.) For an extra special touch, brush with melted butter just before baking.

STICKY PULL-APART BUNS

1 small pkg. regular butterscotch pudding mix
1 C brown sugar, packed
1 C chopped walnuts
4 T butter, softened
1 tsp. ground cinnamon
2 -16 oz. loaves frozen bread dough, thawed

In mixing bowl, combine pudding mix, walnuts, sugar, butter and cinnamon. Stir until crumbly. Cut each loaf of dough in half, lengthwise, then into 8 pieces crosswise (for 16 pieces per loaf). Sprinkle ¼ of topping mix into each of two greased 9X5X4" loaf pans. Arrange 16 dough pieces in each pan. Sprinkle each with half of the remaining topping mix. Cover and let raise in a warm place until almost doubled, about 1 hour. Bake at 350° for 35 to 40 minutes. Turn out of pans onto serving plates immediately. Serve warm.

ONE DISH CINNAMON SWIRL*

Batter:
1½ C all purpose flour
¼ C granulated sugar
¼ tsp salt
2 envelopes quick rise yeast
2/3 C warm (120°) milk
2 T butter, melted
2 T vegetable oil
1 egg, lightly beaten
Cinnamon Mixture:
3 T butter, softened
¾ C light brown sugar
1½ tsp ground cinnamon
Icing:
1 C powdered sugar
1 – 2 T milk
2 T butter, melted
½ tsp vanilla

Mix batter ingredients in a non-stick sprayed 8X8" baking dish; let rest for 10 minutes. Combine cinnamon mixture in a small bowl with a fork and top batter evenly with cinnamon mixture. Using fingers, poke topping thoroughly into batter. Bake, by first placing into a cold oven; setting temperature to 350° and bake for 25 to 30 minutes, until lightly browned and firm in center. Cool 10 minutes. Combine icing ingredients and drizzle over warm cake. *I found this recipe in an old coupon ad (for Fleischman and C&H) and it sounded perfect for the RV life.

BATTER BUNS

2/3 C warm (110-115^0) water
¼ C shortening
1 pkg. active dry yeast
1 egg, beaten
2 T sugar
1 2/3 C flour
½ tsp. salt

Measure warm water into mixing bowl. Add yeast, stirring until dissolved. Add sugar, salt, shortening, egg, and 1 C of the flour. Combine with mixer on low. Stir in remaining flour. Stir until smooth. Spoon into greased muffin cups ½ full. Let rise in warm place for 30 – 40 minutes. Bake at 375° for 18 – 20 minutes until golden brown.

HAM & SWISS BRAID

4 C all purpose flour
2 T butter
2 T sugar
1 lb. thinly sliced deli ham
2 pkg. quick rise yeast
1 C (4 oz) shredded Swiss cheese
½ tsp salt
½ C chopped dill pickles or relish, optional
1 C water
1 egg, lightly beaten
¼ C Dijon mustard

In a large bowl, combine 3 C flour, sugar, yeast, and salt. In a small saucepan, heat water, mustard, and butter to 120 degrees. Add to flour mixture and mix well. Stir in enough of the remaining flour to form a soft dough. Turn out onto a floured surface and knead until smooth and elastic (6-8 minutes). Roll dough out to a 14 X 12" rectangle on a greased baking sheet. In the center 1/3, arrange ½ of the ham over dough. Top with cheese, pickles, then remaining ham. On each remaining 1/3, cut ¾" wide strips from the outer edge to about 2½" in, toward the center. Starting at one end, fold alternate strips at an angle over filling. Pinch ends to seal. (It will look braided.) Cover and let rise for 15-30 minutes. Gently brush with beaten egg and bake at 375° for 30-35 minutes, until golden brown. Serve warm. This goes together quickly and is good, chilled or wrapped in foil and reheated in a moderate oven, if you have any leftovers.

BREAKFASTS

BAKED EGGS

4 thin slices bread, crusts trimmed
4 eggs
2 T butter at room temperature
salt and pepper, to taste
¼ - ½ C shredded cheddar cheese, opt.
4 tsp salsa, optional*

Lightly spread butter on both sides of bread slices and gently press down into 3" muffin cups. Bake at 350º for 10 – 12 minutes until lightly browned. Remove from oven and carefully break one egg into each cup. Bake for additional 15 – 17 minutes. Top with shredded cheddar and salsa, if desired, and continue baking until cheese is melted and eggs are set. *1 or 2 T diced bacon, ham, onions, peppers, etc. make good options, too!

BANANA PECAN BUTTERMILK PANCAKES

1 egg

1 C buttermilk

2 T melted butter or vegetable oil

2 T sugar

½ tsp salt

2 tsp baking powder

1 tsp baking soda

1¼ C all purpose flour

½ C chopped pecans

1 ripe banana, cut in half lengthwise, then across again lengthwise, then into 1/4" slices

In a 1½ qt. bowl, whisk egg and add buttermilk. Whisk in melted butter or oil and sugar, then salt, baking powder, and soda. When combined well, add flour and whisk until smooth. (May add additional buttermilk, 1 – 2 T, if batter is too thick.) Stir in banana and pecans and spoon onto a heated, lightly oiled skillet by ¼ to ½ cupfulls. Do not spread batter or crowd in pan. Flip to other side when bubbles appear and bottom has browned, and cook until other side is also nicely browned. Serve, buttered, with maple syrup if desired. Makes 7 or 8 - 4" pancakes. Leave out bananas and pecans for plain buttermilk pancakes and/or add in blueberries (fresh or frozen) or sliced strawberries for a different treat.

BLENDER APPLE PANCAKES

Recipe per person:

Break one egg into blender. Turn on and quickly off. Add 1 T melted butter, 1 tsp. baking powder, and ½ C milk or buttermilk. Pulse on and off. Add 1 small peeled, finely diced apple and 1 tsp sugar. Pulse on and off. Add 1 C flour, a little at a time until blender starts to slow down. Cook on lightly oiled griddle, over medium heat for about one minute per side. Butter lightly, if desired. Good even without syrup.

SIMPLE VANILLA CREPES

1 C milk

2 T powdered sugar, plus more for dusting

2 eggs, beaten well

¼ tsp salt

1 T real vanilla

3 T melted butter, cooled, plus more, to cook

¾ C all purpose flour

½ C fruit preserves, heated

Whisk together the beaten eggs, milk, and vanilla. Mix together the flour, powdered sugar, and salt and add to mixture, whisking until smooth, then whisk in the melted butter. ** Set aside to rest for 15 minutes. Meanwhile, heat a well seasoned, or non-stick, skillet over medium heat until hot. Place ½ tsp of butter into the skillet (or spray with non-stick spray) and quickly pour a scant ¼ C (I use a ¼ C measuring cup) batter into the hot skillet, tipping the skillet gently to evenly spread batter. When top looks dry, after 30 - 45 seconds, gently flip over (I use a silicone spatula to gently lift and turn.) and cook other side until edges are golden brown. Transfer to a plate and repeat process, rolling up the first crepe as the next one cooks. Dust with powdered sugar, and serve with your favorite jam or preserves, heated until syrupy. (Place jam in a micro-safe dish and heat for 30 - 45 seconds on high.) This is a great way to use up those jams you couldn't resist at the last gift shop you visited. My favorite is seedless blackberry jam. Enough for 2 people. **(Or place all ingredients, except preserves, in blender and process until smooth.)

FUNNEL CAKES

1 egg
1½ C all purpose flour
½ C milk
3 T sugar
½ C water
1½ tsp baking powder
½ tsp vanilla
1/8 tsp salt
Vegetable oil for frying
Powdered sugar, whipped cream, and sliced, sweetened strawberries or other fruit for serving.

In small mixing bowl, beat egg. Add milk, water, and vanilla. Mix well. Combine dry ingredients and beat into egg mixture until smooth. Heat oil in skillet or fryer to 375°. Pour ½ C from measuring cup into hot oil, forming a spiral. Fry for 2 minutes on each side until golden brown. Drain on paper towels, then dust with powdered sugar and serve with fruit and whipped cream. (Recipe can be doubled.)

BROWNED BUTTER FRESH BLUEBERRY MUFFINS

(Adapted from joythebaker.com, who adapted from The Gourmet Cookbook)
7 T unsalted butter
1/3 C whole milk
1 large egg
1 large egg yolk
1 tsp pure vanilla extract
2 C all purpose flour
½ C white granulated sugar
½ C dark brown sugar, packed
2 tsp baking powder
¾ tsp salt
2 C fresh blueberries (frozen are okay, do not thaw)
1 T fresh lemon juice
1 tsp freshly grated lemon zest
For the Topping:
3 T cold, unsalted butter, cut into 1/2" cubes

½ C all purpose flour

3½ T white granulated sugar

Preheat oven to 375° (convection to 350°). Spray muffin pan or line with paper or foil cups. Melt butter in a small saucepan over medium heat, cooking until little brown flecks appear in the pan. Watch carefully, the crackling will subside and butter will brown very quickly after that. Remove from heat and cool slightly. Whisk milk, egg, yolk, vanilla, lemon juice and zest until combined. Stir in the browned butter. Whisk together flour, sugar, baking powder, and salt in a medium bowl. Add milk and butter mixture all at once and stir gently to combine. Gently, but thoroughly, fold in the blueberries and divide among the muffin cups. Use a fork to press and stir topping ingredients until crumbly. Sprinkle over batter in cups and bake until golden and crisp and a wooden toothpick inserted into middle of a muffin comes out clean, about 18 - 20 minutes. Cool in pan for 10 minutes, then remove from pan. Makes 12- 14 muffins.

OLD FASHIONED SOUTHERN SCRAPPLE

½ lb. bulk pork sausage

1 tsp black pepper

4 C water

1/8 tsp cayenne (red) pepper

1 C (dry) grits

3 T butter (up to ¼ C, to taste)

1 tsp salt

1 C shredded cheddar cheese

Cook sausage until browned; drain. In a heavy saucepan, bring water to a boil. Gradually add grits, salt, pepper, and cayenne. Cook, stirring constantly, until thickened and smooth. Remove from heat and stir in butter and cheese until melted, then stir in sausage. Spoon into a greased loaf pan, smoothing top. Cover and refrigerate for at least 1 hour, or overnight. Turn out of pan and cut into ½" thick slices. Fry in skillet in butter or oil until browned on both sides to serve as a side dish, along with a freshly steamed vegetable, for ribs, or as a breakfast food, served with warm syrup. Good old southern comfort food.

SAUSAGE GRAVY FOR BISCUITS AND GRAVY

1 lb. pkg. bulk sausage
¼ C all purpose flour
½ tsp thyme
½ tsp sage
1 tsp freshly ground black pepper
½ tsp salt, or to taste
1/8 tsp cayenne, optional
1½ - 2 C milk

In a large heavy skillet, over medium high heat, break up sausage and cook, stirring often, until thoroughly and evenly brown. Sprinkle flour over sausage and its drippings, and continue stirring and cooking just until flour begins to brown. Immediately reduce heat to medium and while stirring, pour in milk. Continue stirring to add in thyme, sage, salt, pepper, and cayenne, if used. Cook for an additional 5 minutes, stirring as needed, and serve over your favorite biscuits for a breakfast treat.

BISCUITS:
2 C flour
2 tsp baking powder
½ tsp baking soda
¼ C cold butter, cut into ½" cubes
1 tsp salt
2/3 C buttermilk

Sift flour, salt, baking soda, and baking powder together. Add butter, cutting in with a fork. Add buttermilk to make a soft dough. Knead just enough to pat into a 1/3" thick rectangle. Cut into 2" circles, shaping and re-cutting cut-offs only once, and place on ungreased baking sheet and bake at 400° for 10 - 12 minutes until golden brown.

BLUEBERRY SMOOTHIE

1 – 8 oz. container plain or vanilla yogurt
½ C unsweetened pineapple juice
1 C frozen blueberries (do not thaw)
½ C light peaches, chopped
3 - 4 ice cubes
1 T honey (or 1 pkt. sweetener)

Place all ingredients for your choice of smoothie in blender and mix until smooth. Will make one or two servings. *I like to buy fresh berries or fruit, in season, and clean and slice if needed, to freeze for these fantastic breakfast treats. Freeze the prepared fruit in a layer, on a pan or cookie sheet that will fit in your freezer, and then seal in a zip-top bag when frozen to use at your convenience. Bagged, the fruit fits nicely in small spaces in your freezer, or you can purchase already prepared frozen fruit.

STRAWBERRY BANANA SMOOTHIE
1 - 8 oz. container plain or vanilla yogurt
½ C orange juice
1 C frozen strawberries (do not thaw)
1 banana, peeled and sliced
2 – 3 ice cubes
1 T honey (or 1 pkt. sweetener)
Place all ingredients in blender and mix until smooth. Will make one or two servings.

BREAKFAST BLENDER SHAKES
1 C orange juice
½ C grapefruit juice
1 ripe banana
½ C vanilla yogurt
½ tsp vanilla
Combine in a blender and process until smooth. Serves 2.
Or
1 C orange juice
½ C yogurt
1 tsp honey
Combine in a blender and process until smooth. Serves 1.

HOT BREAKFAST JUICE REFRESHER
3 C orange juice
1 C grapefruit juice
½ C honey
1 cinnamon stick
Combine in a small saucepan. Stir and heat until hot, but do not boil.
Remove cinnamon stick before serving. Serves 3 or 4.

HOT COCOA MIX
2 C powdered (coffee) creamer
1½ C sugar
¾ C unsweetened baking cocoa
½ C powdered milk
¼ tsp salt
Combine all ingredients and mix well. Store in a large airtight container.
To serve, spoon 2 to 3 heaping tsp into mug. Add 1 C boiling water and
stir well.

PANCAKE SYRUP
1 C white sugar
1 C brown sugar, packed
1 C water
¼ tsp maple flavoring
dash salt
Combine sugars, dash salt, and water in a heavy saucepan. Cook over
medium heat, stirring until sugar dissolves. Let mixture come up to a boil
and cook, uncovered, boiling gently for five minutes. Remove from heat
and stir in maple flavoring. Let cool slightly before using. Makes 2 C.

CASHEW NUT MILK
¾ - 1 C raw cashews
3 large Medjool dates, seeds removed
dash salt
½ tsp vanilla, optional
7 – 8 C filtered water

1 quart glass jar with lid

Put cashews in jar and fill with filtered water. Cap and refrigerate overnight. The following day, pour off soaking water and put cashews into a blender container with 3 C filtered water, dates, salt and vanilla. With cover on, blenderize on high for several minutes until completely smooth. Store, covered, in refrigerator for as much as a week. Use on cereal, in smoothies, and as a substitute for regular milk. Shake well before using. (I found a plastic blender bottle at the grocery that has a wire ball inside for mixing and a lidded pour spout that works very well for convenient storage and use.) I love this milk!

CAKES & SWEET TREATS

CHOCOLATE CHIP DESSERT CHEESE BALL

1 – 8 oz. pkg. cream cheese, softened
2 T brown sugar
½ C butter, softened (1 cube)
¾ C mini semi-sweet chocolate morsels
¼ tsp vanilla
¾ C finely chopped pecans
¾ C powdered sugar

Beat cream cheese, butter, and vanilla until fluffy. Gradually add sugars; beat just until combined. Place mixture on a large piece of plastic wrap, use wrap to shape mixture into a ball and cover, and then chill for at least 1 hour. Just before serving, roll cheese ball in chopped pecans. Serve with regular and chocolate graham crackers.

PUMPKIN PIE CAKE

1 large (28 oz.) can pumpkin (not pie filling!)
1½ C sugar
4 eggs, beaten
½ tsp ground cloves
1 tsp ground ginger
1 large (12 oz.) can evaporated milk
1 yellow cake mix
1 C (2 cubes) butter, melted
1½ C chopped walnuts

Mix together pumpkin, sugar, eggs, cloves, ginger, and evaporated milk and pour into a greased 9X13X2" pan. Sprinkle cake mix evenly over pumpkin batter in pan. Drizzle melted butter evenly over cake mix. Sprinkle walnuts over all and bake at 375⁰ for 30 minutes. Reduce heat to 350⁰ and bake for 60 minutes more. Let cool before cutting.

OATMEAL CAKE WITH COCONUT-PECAN FROSTING

1 C boiling water

1 C oats, quick or old fashioned

½ C butter

1 C sugar

1 C brown sugar, packed

2 eggs, beaten

1¼ C flour

1 tsp baking soda

1 tsp salt

½ tsp nutmeg

1 tsp cinnamon

Pour boiling water over oats and butter and let stand for 20 minutes. Add sugars and mix well. Blend in eggs and vanilla. Sift together flour, soda, salt, cinnamon, and nutmeg and add to creamed mixture. Mix well. Pour batter into greased and floured 9 X 9" pan. Bake for 50 – 55 minutes in a preheated 350⁰ oven until done. Remove from oven and turn oven to broil. Do not remove cake from pan. Prepare frosting.

6 T butter, soft

1 tsp vanilla

½ C evaporated milk

1 C shredded coconut

½ C sugar

1 C chopped pecans

Cream together butter, sugar, and vanilla; mix in evaporated milk until combined and stir in coconut and pecans. Spoon mixture over still warm cake and place pan in oven to broil until coconut and nuts are toasty brown, watching carefully to prevent burning.

QUICK & EASY CHOCOLATE CAKE

1½ C flour
1 C sugar
¼ C cocoa
½ tsp salt
1 tsp baking soda
1 tsp vanilla
1 T vinegar
1/3 C vegetable oil
1 C cold water, coffee, OR milk

Preheat oven to 350^0. Spray an 8" square or 9" round pan, at least 2" deep, with non-stick spray. Whisk together all of the dry ingredients in a bowl. Make three indentations and in the first, pour vanilla, in the second, pour the vinegar, and in the third, pour the vegetable oil. Take the cup of cold liquid and pour it over all. Whisk all ingredients together until well blended. Pour into prepared pan and bake for 30-35 minutes until done. Serve warm, directly from pan. Sprinkle with powdered sugar, if desired.

CHOCOLATE MAYONNAISE CAKE WITH CARAMEL FROSTING

2 C flour
1 C sugar
3 T cocoa
2 tsp baking soda
1 C water
1 C mayonnaise
1 tsp vanilla
Caramel Frosting
¼ C butter
½ C brown sugar, packed
1 ¾ C powdered sugar
2 T milk

Combine dry ingredients for cake in a mixing bowl. Add water, mayonnaise, and vanilla and beat until blended. Pour into a greased 9" square pan and bake at 350^0 for 30-35 minutes or until a toothpick inserted into center of cake comes out clean. For frosting, melt butter in saucepan. Add in brown sugar and cook, stirring until it comes up to a boil. Remove from heat and carefully stir in milk. Gradually beat in powdered sugar by hand until frosting consistency. Immediately frost cake.

$450 CAKE WITH VANILLA CREAM FROSTING

1 tsp baking soda
1 tsp water
1 oz. (1 bottle) red food coloring
2 T cocoa
1½ C sugar
½ C butter
2 eggs
2½ C flour
1 T baking powder
1 tsp salt
1 C buttermilk
1 T vanilla

Mix baking soda and water in small cup and set aside. In another small cup, combine red food color and cocoa and set aside. Cream together butter and sugar and add in eggs and soda/water mix and red color/cocoa mix. In a separate bowl, whisk together flour, baking powder, and salt. Add to butter/sugar mixture, alternating with buttermilk and then stir in vanilla. Pour into a non-stick sprayed 9x13x2" baking pan or 3 – 8" round pans. Bake in a preheated 350⁰ oven for 35-40 minutes or until toothpick inserted in middle comes out clean. For frosting:

3 T flour
1 C milk
1 C butter
1 C sugar
1 T flour
1 T vanilla

Boil together 3 T flour and milk until thick and let cool completely. Beat together 1 C butter, sugar, and 1 T flour. Add in vanilla and cooled white sauce. Beat until thickened and use to frost cooled cake.

SOUR CREAM POUND CAKE

3 C sugar
1 C (2 sticks) butter, out of refrigerator for 20 minutes
1 C sour cream
¼ tsp baking soda
6 eggs, at room temperature
3 C flour
1 tsp vanilla
½ tsp lemon extract

Cream together butter and sugar until light and fluffy. Add soda, sour cream, and flavorings and mix well. Beat in eggs, two at a time, alternating with 1 C flour, until all eggs and flour have been added, beating well after each addition. Pour into a buttered tube or Bundt pan or two buttered 5X9" loaf pans and bake at 325⁰ for 90 minutes. Cool in pans on rack for 15 minutes, then turn out to cool completely.

PUMPKIN BREAD

2 C all purpose flour
1 tsp baking soda
½ tsp baking powder
½ tsp salt
1½ tsp ground cinnamon
¼ tsp each ground cloves and ground nutmeg
½ tsp ground cardamom
½ C (1 stick) unsalted butter, at room temperature
1¼ C brown sugar, packed
3 large eggs
1 T vanilla
1 – 15 oz. can pumpkin puree (not pie filling!)
Optional: ½ C chopped walnuts, and/or ½ C golden raisins
White sugar for dusting pan
Preheat oven to 350° (325° for convection). Whisk together dry ingredients and spices in a medium bowl. In large bowl, cream together butter and brown sugar. Beat in eggs, one at a time, until light and fluffy. Stir in vanilla and pumpkin. Add flour mixture and beat just until combined. Stir in nuts and/or raisins. Butter a Bundt pan or 2 - 8X4" loaf pans and sprinkle 2-3 T white sugar into pan(s), shaking to coat bottom and sides well. Pour in batter and bake for approximately 1 hour (45 minutes for smaller loaves) or until a toothpick, inserted into center of loaf, comes out clean. Cool 15 minutes in pan, then remove and cool completely before slicing.

ZUCCHINI BREAD

3 eggs, well beaten
1 C vegetable oil
2 C sugar
2 C grated zucchini
3 C flour
½ tsp baking powder
1 tsp baking soda
2 T vanilla
1 tsp salt
1 C chopped nuts, if desired
3 tsp ground cinnamon

Mix eggs, vanilla, and oil in large mixing bowl. Combine dry ingredients together and stir into egg mixture. Add grated zucchini and chopped nuts and stir just until combined. Spray two loaf pans or one Bundt pan with non-stick spray and bake at 350° for 1 hour. Cool in pan for 15 minutes, then turn onto rack and cool completely.

BANANA NUT BREAD

½ C + 2 T butter, browned and cooled completely
1 C sugar
2 eggs
1 tsp vanilla
2¼ C flour
2 tsp baking powder
½ tsp baking soda
¾ tsp salt
2 T buttermilk
1½ C ripe bananas, lightly mashed
¾ C walnuts or pecans, chopped

In a small sauce pan over medium heat, slowly melt butter, and watching carefully, let it begin to brown, and as it browns and emits a nice nutty smell, remove from heat and pour into a heat proof bowl or measuring cup. Let cool completely until it begins to set up again. When cool, spoon out into a mixing bowl and cream together with sugar. Beat in eggs and vanilla. Combine flour, baking powder, soda, and salt, and alternating with bananas and buttermilk, stir into butter mixture, beating until smooth. Spray a Bundt pan (or 2 loaf pans) with non-stick spray and pour in batter. Bake at 350⁰ in a pre-heated oven for 55 – 60 minutes, or until a toothpick inserted in center of cake comes out clean. Cool in pan for 10 minutes and turn out onto a cooling rack. When cooled, shake powdered sugar over for a pretty presentation.

MAGICALLY MOIST GLUTEN-FREE ALMOND CAKE

¾ C unsalted butter

1 C sugar

4 eggs

½ C milk

1 tsp vanilla

1½ C almond meal (almond flour)

½ C coconut flour (this adds great flavor and fiber)

¼ tsp salt

2 tsp baking powder

Cream together butter and sugar until smooth. Add in eggs, one at a time, and beat until fully blended. Add milk and vanilla, and mix until combined. In a separate bowl, combine flours, salt, and baking powder. Add the dry ingredients into the wet ingredients and beat until creamy. Spread in a greased 9 x 13 cake pan and bake at 350⁰ for 30 minutes. This delightfully rich cake is a wonderful base for fresh mixed berries, lightly sweetened, and topped with whipped cream. Chill leftovers. Many thanks to my sister, Dani Weber, gluten-free for many years, for this recipe.

DUMP CAKE

1 can cherry pie filling

1 can crushed pineapple

1 yellow cake mix

1 C chopped pecans

1 C (2 cubes) butter, cut in pats

Layer items in order in a 9" square pan sprayed with non-stick spray. Do NOT stir and do NOT peek! Bake at 350⁰ for 1 hour. Let cool before cutting and serving. So simple and so good!

BLUEBERRY DESSERT

32 vanilla wafers, crushed
2 eggs
½ C butter, melted
1 tsp vanilla
¼ C sugar
1 can blueberry pie filling
1 - 8oz. pkg. cream cheese, softened
½ C sugar
1 - 8 oz. tub frozen whipped topping, thawed

Combine crushed wafers, melted butter, and ¼ C sugar. Pat into bottom of 11 X 7" pan. Mix cream cheese, ½ C sugar, eggs, and vanilla. Pour cheese mixture over crumb base and bake in a preheated 375° oven for 20 minutes. When cool, spread blueberry pie filling over cheese mixture and frost with whipped topping. Chill until ready to serve, and cut into squares for serving.

PEACH CRUNCH KUCHEN

1 C all purpose flour
¼ tsp ground nutmeg
½ tsp salt
1 large can sliced peaches, drained
½ C sugar
4 eggs
1/3 C butter
1 C sour cream
½ tsp ground cinnamon

Combine flour, salt, and 2 T sugar in mixing bowl. Fluff with a fork or whisk, then cut in butter until crumbly. Reserve ¼ C for topping and press remaining mixture into a 9" square pan. Combine remaining sugar with cinnamon and nutmeg. Arrange peach slices in pan and sprinkle with 2 T of the sugar mixture. Bake at 400° for 15 minutes. Remove from oven and reduce heat to 350°. Beat eggs until light and fluffy. Add sour cream and beat, just until blended. Pour over hot peaches. Combine remaining cinnamon sugar mixture with reserved flour mixture. Sprinkle over all. Bake for additional 25 minutes, until knife inserted into center comes out clean. Serve warm, with ice cream or whipped cream.

BLUEBERRY BUCKLE

¼ C shortening
2 tsp baking powder
¾ C sugar
½ tsp salt
1 egg
½ C milk
2 C flour
2 C fresh or frozen blueberries
Topping:
½ C flour
1/3 C sugar
½ tsp cinnamon
¼ C cold butter, cut into pats

Cream shortening and sugar together. Beat in egg; mix well. Combine flour, baking powder, and salt; add alternately with milk, mixing well. Fold in berries and pour into a greased 9" square pan. For topping: combine sugar, flour, and cinnamon. Cut in butter to coarse crumbs. Sprinkle over batter. Bake at 350° for 45 minutes until toothpick comes out clean. Cool for 10 minutes before cutting. (If using frozen berries, do not thaw.)

MICROWAVE RAISIN BREAD PUDDING WITH VANILLA OR RUM SAUCE

7 slices raisin bread
¼ C brown sugar
2 C milk
¼ C butter
2 eggs, lightly beaten
1 tsp vanilla
2 T sugar

Cut raisin bread into cubes and spread in buttered 8 X 8" microwave dish. Sprinkle with brown sugar. Microwave milk and butter on high in a 4 C glass bowl for 4 minutes. Whisk beaten eggs and sugar into milk mixture and pour over bread cubes. Press bread down into mixture. Microwave on high for 8½ to 9 minutes, until knife inserted into center comes out clean. Serves 9.

VANILLA (OR RUM) SAUCE FOR RAISIN BREAD PUDDING:

½ C butter

1 C sugar

1 egg

2 T vanilla (or rum flavoring)

Cream together butter and sugar. Stir in beaten egg. Heat over medium heat in a small heavy saucepan until melted, then turn down to low and stir constantly for 5 minutes. Add flavoring and serve warm over pudding. Submitted by Rose Hager. (She notes that this is a quick generator run to use the microwave when you are boondocking.)

OLD FASHIONED RICE PUDDING

¾ C raw white rice (short grain or Arborio rice works best)

¾ C sugar

2 C whole milk

1 C heavy cream

1 T vanilla

½ tsp cinnamon

¼ tsp nutmeg

4 eggs, beaten

In large pot, heat rice and milk just to boiling. Cover and simmer until rice is done (about ½ hour), stirring now and then. While rice is simmering, beat together eggs, sugar, vanilla, cinnamon, and nutmeg. When rice is tender, add egg mixture to pot gradually, whisking constantly. Bring mixture to a boil, stirring for a minute or two to thicken. Serve warm or chill. Garnish with whipped cream and additional cinnamon, if desired.

CHIFFON PUDDING

¼ C fresh lemon juice
2 T cornstarch
½ C sugar (or 12 packets sweetener)
1½ C cool water

In heavy bottomed 1 qt. saucepan, whisk together water and cornstarch. Add remaining ingredients and bring to a boil over medium heat, whisking constantly until thick. Add more sweetening, if desired. Chill and serve with whipped cream or topping.

DREAMSICLE PUDDING

1 small box instant fat and sugar free vanilla pudding mix
1 small can mandarin oranges, drained-reserve the juice
1- 8 oz. tub fat free frozen whipped topping, thawed
1 small box sugar free orange gelatin

Add enough water to reserved juice to make 1 C. Bring to a boil in 1 qt. saucepan. Remove from heat and stir in gelatin until dissolved. Add 3 ice cubes to a measuring cup and fill to 1 C with cold water. Stir into gelatin until melted and set aside to cool for 5 minutes. Transfer to a mixing bowl and with electric mixer, beat in dry pudding mix until well mixed. Fold in the whipped topping and then the mandarin oranges. Chill until set, at least 3 hours or overnight. Submitted by Pat Lewis.

FROZEN LEMON MOUSSE

1 tsp grated lemon zest
¼ C freshly squeezed lemon juice
4 T unsalted butter, chilled and cubed
4 large egg yolks
¾ C heavy cream
5 T white sugar

Whisk together lemon juice and zest, egg yolks, and sugar in a small heavy saucepan. Cook, whisking constantly, over medium/low heat until mixture thickens. (5-6 minutes.) Remove from heat, add butter and stir until melted. Cover with plastic wrap, pressing it down to touch surface (to prevent a skin forming). Chill for at least 30 minutes. Whip cream to stiff peaks and fold into lemon mixture until combined. Divide into paper lined cupcake pan, OR 6 – 4 oz. ramekins, OR a prepared graham cracker piecrust and freeze for 2 hours. Serve with whipped cream if desired.

HOMEMADE CHOCOLATE PUDDING

1 C sugar
½ C cocoa
¼ C cornstarch
½ tsp salt
4 C milk
2 T butter
2 tsp vanilla

In heavy saucepan, whisk together sugar, cocoa, cornstarch, and salt. Gradually whisk in milk and bring to a rolling boil over medium heat. Boil, stirring constantly, for 2 minutes until thickened. Remove from heat and stir in butter and vanilla. Serve warm or chill.

PEACHES AND CREAM PIZZA

1 -14 oz. can sweetened condensed milk
½ C sour cream
¼ C lemon juice
1 tsp vanilla
½ C butter, softened
¼ C brown sugar, packed
1 C flour
¼ C quick cooking oats
¼ C walnuts, finely chopped
1 - 29 oz. can peach slices, well drained

In medium mixing bowl, cream together sweetened condensed milk, sour cream, lemon juice, and vanilla. Cover with plastic and chill. In another medium bowl, cream butter and sugar until light and fluffy. Stir in flour, oats, and walnuts until thoroughly blended. Spray a 12" pizza pan with non-stick spray and press oat mixture gently onto pan, forming a slight ridge around pan edge. Prick 5 or 6 times with a fork and bake for 10 - 12 minutes in a preheated 375° oven until golden brown. Cool completely and spread chilled cream filling carefully over cookie crust. Arrange drained peaches decoratively over cookie crust and keep chilled until ready to serve. Garnish with more chopped walnuts if desired.

STRAWBERRY PIZZA

6 T butter, softened
½ C sugar
1 egg
1 tsp vanilla
½ tsp almond extract
1½ C flour
½ tsp baking powder
½ tsp baking soda
½ tsp salt

Cream butter and sugar together. When fluffy, add in egg and add flavorings. Combine flour, baking powder, baking soda, and salt and add to creamed mixture. Stir just until combined. Quickly press onto an ungreased 12-14" pizza pan, building up the outside edge. Bake at 350° for 20 minutes, until golden brown. Cool completely! In a mixing bowl, cream together 1

– 8 oz. pkg. softened cream cheese and ½ C powdered sugar. Spread over cooled cookie crust. Arrange 2 C sliced strawberries on top of cream cheese mixture (Can add 1 C fresh blueberries for a red, white, & blue treat!) and top with a glaze of 1 C strawberry jam that has been warmed slightly in the microwave*. Chill thoroughly and slice as for pizza to serve. Enjoy on same day as made as the juice from the berries can soften the cookie base. *OR Combine 2 C crushed strawberries, 1 C sugar, and ¼ C cornstarch in small saucepan and bring to a boil over medium-high heat. Cook for 2 minutes or until thickened. Cool completely and spoon over strawberries on pizza.

FRESH CHERRY CRISP
Mix together in a bowl and set aside:
5 C fresh (or frozen) pitted cherries
1 T cornstarch
½ C light brown sugar
2 T lemon juice (preferably fresh)
In a separate bowl, mix together:
6 T all purpose flour
1½ C old-fashioned oats (quick oats are okay, but not instant)
6 T light brown sugar
½ tsp baking powder
½ tsp salt
¼ tsp ground ginger
¼ tsp ground cinnamon
Cut in 8 T (1/2 C) unsalted butter to coarse, crumbly cookie dough texture. Butter an 8X8" baking pan and fill with cherry mixture. Top with crumble mixture and bake at 375° for 30 minutes until golden brown and juices have thickened. Serve warm and top with fresh whipped cream or ice cream, if desired.

FRIED APPLES

2 crisp, tart apples, peeled, cored, and sliced ¼" thick as for pie
2 T butter
2 T brown sugar
½ tsp cinnamon
1 tsp granulated sugar
Melt butter in a heavy skillet over medium heat. Place apples in an even layer and top with sugars. Cover and cook for 2 minutes. Gently stir and top with cinnamon. Cook only until crisp tender and sugars are melted. Top with cream, whipped cream, or ice cream, and serve warm.

EASY APPLE BUTTER IN A CROCKPOT

Depending on how much you want to make, for every 2 cups of applesauce, add 1 cup of white sugar, ¼ tsp ground cloves, 1 tsp ground cinnamon, and a scant dash of allspice. Stir together in your crockpot and cook on high for approximately 8 hours to thicken. If you want to start from scratch, peel, core, and quarter 4 - 6 apples. Put apples in a microwave dish and add 1T water. Cover with plastic, folding back a corner to vent, and cook on high for 2-3 minutes or just until tender. Mash with a fork and measure out 2 C applesauce and proceed with apple butter recipe. Submitted by Margaret Marks.

MOM'S QUICK FRUIT BAKE

1 C fresh or frozen sliced peaches
1½ C fresh or frozen blueberries
½ to 2/3 C sugar
1 T lemon juice
Combine in a saucepan and bring to a boil. Carefully pour into 9" baking pan. Quickly prepare topping before fruit has time to cool:
1 C sugar
1 cube butter (½ C), at room temperature
1 egg
1 C flour
pinch of salt
Cream sugar and butter until fluffy. Add egg & mix well, then add flour and salt. Mix until all is blended and drop dough by spoonful onto hot

fruit, covering fruit as much as possible. Bake at 375° degrees for 35 to 40 minutes. (Regular or convection oven.) Serve warm. Top with ice cream if you desire, but it is very rich. This is great, made with any of your favorite berries or fruit combinations.

APPLE DUMPLINGS

2 Granny Smith apples
¾ C butter, no substitutions
1½ C sugar
1 tsp vanilla
1 tsp cinnamon
2 cans crescent roll dough
1½ C Mountain Dew

Peel and slice apples into 8 slices each. Microwave for 1-2 minutes. Melt butter and mix with sugar, vanilla, and cinnamon. Roll each slice of apple in a crescent roll dough section and place in a 9" x 13" pan sprayed with non-stick spray. Spread sugar mixture on top and around dumplings. Pour Mountain Dew over all. Bake at 350° for 35 minutes or until golden brown. Submitted by Donna Fischer.

NO BAKE LEMON CHEESECAKE

3 C graham cracker crumbs
½ C melted butter
1/3 C sugar
1 C boiling water
1- 3 oz. pkg. lemon flavor gelatin
3 T lemon juice
1 – 8 oz. pkg. cream cheese, at room temperature
1 C sugar
1 tsp vanilla
1 – 12 oz. can evaporated milk, chilled

Combine graham cracker crumbs with 1/3 C sugar. Stir in melted butter and press into a 9X13" pan, reserving ½ C for garnish. Bake at 350° for 8 minutes, then cool completely and chill while preparing filling. For filling, stir in and completely dissolve gelatin in boiling water. Add lemon juice and chill while making cream cheese mixture. In medium mixing bowl, beat cream cheese, sugar, and vanilla until smooth and fluffy. Set aside. In a large mixing bowl, beat cold evaporated milk on medium high until thickened (2 min.). Beat in cream cheese mixture and cooled gelatin mixture on low speed just until combined. Pour mixture over chilled crust and sprinkle reserved crumbs over top. Cover and chill until set.

QUICK NO BAKE CREAM-CHEESECAKE

1 9" prepared graham cracker piecrust
1- 8 oz. pkg. cream cheese, at room temperature
1 can sweetened condensed milk
½ C bottled or fresh (my preference) lemon juice
1 can prepared cherry (or blueberry, strawberry, etc.) pie filling, optional

Using an electric mixer, beat softened cream cheese until smooth. Pour in sweetened condensed milk and continue mixing while slowly pouring in the lemon juice. Spoon mixture into prepared crust and chill for 2 hours or until firm. Spoon cherry topping over and continue chilling until time to serve. Chill leftovers. **Note: To make this into a simple (Key) Lime cheesecake, substitute bottled or fresh key or regular lime juice and lime zest for lemon and serve with fresh raspberries. Yum!!

RASPBERRY BROWNIE TREATS

Brownie:
½ C butter
1¼ C semisweet chocolate chips
2 eggs
¾ C brown sugar, packed
1 tsp instant coffee granules
½ tsp baking powder
¾ C flour
2 T water
Topping:
1 C semisweet chocolate chips
1 8-oz pkg. cream cheese, softened
¼ C powdered sugar
1/3 C seedless raspberry jam
Glaze:
¼ C semisweet chocolate chips
1 T shortening

For brownie: Melt butter and chocolate chips and let cool. Beat eggs with brown sugar. Dissolve coffee granules in water and add to egg mixture with chocolate. Blend well. Combine baking powder and flour. Stir into chocolate mixture. Bake at 350° for 30 to 35 minutes, in a non-stick sprayed 9X9" baking pan. For topping: Melt chocolate chips, cool slightly and spread over warm brownies. Beat cream cheese until fluffy. Mix powdered sugar and jam into cream cheese, then gently spread over cooled brownies. For glaze: Melt chips and shortening together and drizzle over all.

FAST NO BAKE CHEESECAKE

1 – 9" prepared graham cracker or chocolate crust
1 – 8 oz. pkg. cream cheese, room temperature
1/3 C sugar
1 – 12 oz. container frozen whipped topping, thawed
1 C (6 oz.) semisweet chocolate chips
1 C milk

Beat cream cheese and sugar until light and smooth. Fold in whipped topping. Melt chocolate chips. Add milk and stir until smooth. Fold chocolate mixture into cream cheese mixture and pour into prepared crust. Chill 3-4 hours or overnight, until firm.

CHERRY CHEESECAKE TARTS

1 can cherry pie filling
1 C sugar
3-8 oz. pkg. cream cheese, softened
4 eggs
2 T vanilla
24 vanilla wafer cookies

Beat together sugar and cream cheese. Stir in eggs, 1 at a time, beating well after each. Add vanilla. Line 24 cups of 2 muffin pans with paper liners and place a vanilla wafer cookie in bottom of each. Pour cream cheese mixture in each cup, filling approximately 2/3 full. Bake in a preheated 350° oven for 15-20 minutes until a toothpick comes out clean. Top each with cherry pie filling when cool. Chill thoroughly. These tarts are very popular at potlucks. Submitted by Noreta Ray and Donna Bennett.

LOW CARB CHEESECAKE

Blend together, until smooth:
1 – 8 oz. pkg. cream cheese, softened (reduced fat works well also)
½ C heavy cream
¼ C Splenda
1 large egg
1 tsp. vanilla
Can add ¼ C sour cream, if you like

Pour equal amounts into a six-portion muffin pan, sprayed generously with cooking spray. Bake at 350° for 15 – 20 minutes until light brown on top. Cool for about 15 minutes, then run a knife around each to loosen. Turn the muffin pan upside down and remove from pan. Cool in refrigerator for 1 – 2 hours. Place one "no sugar added" cherry on top of each and serve. Each one has less than 5 carbs. Submitted by Sandy Baleria.

RASPBERRY DECADENCE

1 box fudge brownie mix
1 can raspberry pie filling
Make up brownie mix per package directions. Spread pie filling into the bottom of a 9" round pan. Spread brownie batter over the top. Bake per package directions until brownies are done. This may take longer then package directions, so test rather than rely on timing. The bottom of the brownie layer will still be slightly gooey, but that makes the chocolate layer a molten layer, which adds to the treat. Cut into wedges while warm and serve with ice cream. Note* If you can find Krusteaz brand brownie mix, all you need to add is water, so all you have to keep on hand is the brownie mix and a can of pie filling. Other flavors like strawberry, cherry, or blackberry are also good. Submitted by Diane Melde.

APPLE CRISP

4-5 Gala or other favorite tart, crisp apples; peeled, cored, and sliced (as for pie)
½ C all purpose flour
¼ C white sugar
3 T fresh lemon juice and 1T water
½ C dark brown sugar, packed
1 tsp ground cinnamon
¼ tsp ground nutmeg
1/8 tsp salt
6 T butter, cut into cubes
1 C old-fashioned oats (quick oats will also work)
1/3 to ½ C chopped walnuts or pecans (optional)

Lightly butter an 8 or 9" square baking pan and place apple slices in an even layer. Drizzle lemon juice and water over apples and sprinkle with white sugar; set aside while you prepare topping mix. Preheat oven (or convection oven) to 375°. In mixing bowl, combine oats, flour, brown sugar, salt, cinnamon and nutmeg. Use a fork or two table knives to cut butter into mixture to large crumble. Stir in nuts, if used. Spoon over apples and bake for 40 minutes, until apples are bubbling and topping is crispy! Enjoy warm with vanilla ice cream or whipped cream.

CHOCOLATE ÉCLAIR DESSERT

2 small pkg. vanilla instant pudding mix
1 – 2 sleeves graham crackers
3 C & 3 T milk, divided
1 can chocolate frosting
½ tub frozen whipped topping, thawed

Beat 3 C milk into the pudding mix as directed on package. Mix in ½ tub whipped topping. Line 9x11" pan with whole graham crackers. Spread ½ of the pudding mixture over graham crackers and repeat layers. Top with third layer of graham crackers. Mix 3 T milk into frosting and spread over all. Chill for 24 hours. This can be increased using 2 large packages of pudding mix, 4½ C milk, additional graham crackers, and 1 (8 oz.) tub whipped topping. The same frosting will cover. Submitted by Joyce Horton.

GLUTEN FREE DARK CHOCOLATE WALNUT BROWNIES

1 C butter

¾ C dark or semisweet chocolate chips

2/3 C unsweetened cocoa powder

1¾ C sugar

1 C gluten-free all purpose flour (*or you can substitute 1¼ cup regular A/P flour)

¾ tsp baking powder

½ tsp salt

1 tsp espresso powder (optional)

1 T vanilla extract

5 eggs

¾ C chopped walnuts

¾ C (real) white chocolate chips

Preheat oven to 350°. Butter a 9x13" baking pan. (I also lined with parchment paper and buttered it, too.) In a small heavy pot over low heat, melt butter and chocolate chips together and remove from heat. Cool. In a separate bowl, combine dry ingredients. When the chocolate/butter mixture has cooled, whisk in the eggs and vanilla. Note: it is important to cool the chocolate/butter mixture or the eggs will cook. Add the dry ingredients and whisk to combine. Stir in the chopped walnuts and white chocolate chips. Pour batter into prepared baking pan. Bake for 35-40 minutes or until a knife inserted into center comes out clean. (I baked for 35 minutes at 350⁰ in a convection oven.) *NOTE This is NOT gluten-free if regular flour is used!!

SNICKERS BROWNIES

1 German chocolate cake mix
1 C chocolate chips
14 oz. caramels, unwrapped
1 C chopped nuts
¾ C melted butter
1 can sweetened condensed milk

Mix the cake mix with ½ of the can of sweetened condensed milk, melted butter, and nuts. Press ½ of this mixture into a 9" X 13" baking pan sprayed with non-stick spray. Bake at 350° for 6 – 8 minutes in a preheated oven. While that is baking, melt caramels with the rest of the sweetened condensed milk. Remove cake from oven and pour caramel mixture over the top. Sprinkle chocolate chips over all then spoon remaining batter over the top of that. It will spread as it bakes. Return to oven and bake for an additional 16 – 18 minutes. Submitted by Barbara Thompkins.

MY FAVORITE BITTERSWEET BROWNIES

1 cube (1/2 C) plus 2 T butter, melted
1 T vanilla
2/3 C cocoa powder
1/3 C flour
1 1/3 C sugar
½ tsp baking powder
2 large eggs, lightly beaten
¼ tsp salt
¾ C broken walnuts, optional

Stir melted butter into sugar in a large mixing bowl. Beat in eggs and vanilla. Stir together flour, salt, baking powder, and cocoa and add to egg mixture. Combine and mix just until blended. Stir in walnuts and pour into a buttered 8X8" square pan. Bake at 350° for 25 minutes. Cool and cut into squares. Makes 16.

ROCKY ROAD BROWNIES

8 – oz. unsweetened chocolate
1 C (2 sticks) butter
5 large eggs, beaten
3½ C sugar
2 tsp espresso powder, optional
1 T vanilla
½ tsp salt
1 2/3 C all purpose flour
1 C semi-sweet chocolate chips or chunks, divided
1 C mini-marshmallows, divided
1 C toasted walnuts, divided

In a heat safe bowl (or in a small pot over med-low heat on the stovetop), gently melt together the butter and unsweetened chocolate in the microwave on high, stirring and checking frequently, first at 1 minute, then at 30-second intervals until just barely melted. Let cool. Beat eggs, stirring in sugar and beating well. Add vanilla, cooled chocolate and butter mixture and combine well. In another bowl, whisk together flour, salt and espresso, if used. Stir into chocolate mixture, just until combined. Fold in ONE HALF of chocolate chips, walnuts, and marshmallows and mix until combined. Pour into a well buttered (or lined with foil and buttered) 9X13" baking pan and bake in a preheated 375° convection oven for 25 minutes. Remove from oven and raise temperature to 400°. Sprinkle top of brownies with remaining half of chips, nuts, and marshmallows. Return to oven and continue baking for additional 8 – 12 minutes or until topping is golden brown to your liking. Cool completely to cut and serve. May take 5 – 10 minutes longer for initial bake in regular oven.

FRITO BARS

1 - 10 oz. (med.) pkg. Fritos chips

1 C sugar

1 C light Karo (corn) syrup

1 C chunky peanut butter

Spread chips in bottom of 9X12" baking pan. In medium saucepan, mix 1 C sugar and 1 C corn syrup. Heat to a rolling boil. Remove from heat and stir in 1 C chunky peanut butter. Mix well and spread over chips. Let this set up for 30 – 45 minutes until cool, then cut into squares to serve. Submitted by Sara Wardlow.

QUICK HOT FUDGE SAUCE

1 – 14 oz. can sweetened condensed milk

4 – 1 oz. squares semisweet chocolate

2 T butter

1 tsp vanilla

Stir together milk, chocolate, and butter in a small heavy saucepan. Cook over medium heat until chocolate is melted. Remove from heat and stir in vanilla. Serve warm over ice cream or pound cake. This can be reheated and when covered, keeps well in the refrigerator for 2-3 weeks.

KAREN'S NEVER FAIL FUDGE

2 C granulated sugar

2 T cocoa

½ C skim milk

1/3 C white corn syrup

1 tsp. butter

1 tsp. Vanilla

1½ C pecans

Stir together sugar and cocoa, and add milk and corn syrup. Cook over medium heat until boiling. Cook 7 minutes without stirring. Remove from heat, add butter, vanilla & pecans, pour into greased 8X6" pan. Submitted by Karen Miller.

EASY FUDGE

74

1 – 16 oz. can vanilla frosting (or any flavor)
1 – 16 oz. pkg. chocolate chips (or any flavor)
1 C chopped nuts (your choice)
Place chips in bottom of microwave safe bowl. Top with frosting and microwave for 1½ minutes. Mix well. Pour into buttered 8X8" square pan and refrigerate for at least one hour. Cut and serve. Submitted by JoAnn Borrousch.

MICROWAVE PECAN BRITTLE

1 C white sugar
1 tsp butter
½ C light corn syrup
1 tsp vanilla
1/8 tsp salt
2 tsp baking soda
1 to 1½ C pecan pieces
foil lined and buttered jelly roll pan
Measure out 2 tsp baking soda; set aside. Measure out 1 tsp butter; set aside. Set out 1 tsp vanilla. In 1 quart micro-safe bowl, combine sugar, corn syrup, salt, and pecans. Cook in microwave oven on high for 4 minutes. Add butter and vanilla. Stir to combine. Cook in microwave on high for 2 minutes. Add baking soda and stir well until mixture foams up and turns golden. Pour onto buttered foil and spread out. Allow to cool and harden. Break into pieces. This makes a foamier, easier to eat brittle.

PRETZEL TREATS

1 small pkg. small salted pretzels
3 – 4 rolls of Rollo chocolate/caramel candies
6 – 8 oz. pecan halves
On a parchment covered pan, spread out pretzels and top each one with one Rollo candy. Place in a preheated 325⁰ oven for 6-8 minutes, watching carefully so that candies don't melt, only soften. Remove from oven and immediately gently press one pecan half onto each candy. Let cool and store in an airtight container.

Miss Terry's Kitchen

CHICKEN

TERRY'S BEST FRIED CHICKEN

3 – 4 bone-in, skin-on chicken breasts
2 – 3 C buttermilk with 1-2 T salt, for marinating
2 C all-purpose flour for coating
3 T cornstarch
1 tsp baking soda
1 tsp smoked paprika
1 tsp crushed rosemary
1 tsp crushed thyme
1 tsp crushed sage
freshly ground sea salt and pepper, to taste
2 quarts vegetable oil for frying
hot pepper sauce, to taste, if desired, added to buttermilk for marinade

Put the flour in a large plastic bag (let the amount of chicken you are cooking dictate the amount of flour you use). Season the flour with smoked paprika, rosemary, thyme, sage, salt and pepper and add the baking soda. Marinate chicken pieces in buttermilk (I use a large zip-top bag, squeezing air out, and place in large bowl in fridge, to protect from leakage) for several hours, or overnight, and then, a few at a time, put them in the bag with the flour, seal the bag and shake to coat well. Place the coated chicken on a cookie sheet or cooling rack over a tray, and cover with a clean dishtowel or waxed paper. Let rest for 10 – 15 minutes. Discard bag and marinade.

Fill a large deep skillet (cast iron is best) about 1/3 to 1/2 full with vegetable oil. Heat until VERY hot. Carefully place as many chicken pieces as the skillet can hold without overfilling. Brown the chicken in HOT oil on both sides. When browned, reduce heat and cover skillet; let cook for 20 minutes (the chicken will be cooked through but not crispy). Remove cover, raise heat again and continue to fry until crispy and brown and juices run clear when pierced with a fork. Drain the fried chicken on paper towels. Depending on how much chicken you have, you may have to fry in a few shifts. Keep the finished chicken in a warm oven while preparing the rest.

LOWFAT BAKED BASIL CHICKEN

1 lb. boneless skinless chicken breasts
1/3 C low-fat plain yogurt
¼ C chopped fresh basil (can use 1T dry)
1 tsp cornstarch
½ C dry breadcrumbs
1 T grated Parmesan cheese
½ tsp each salt and freshly ground pepper

Arrange chicken in a single layer in a sprayed baking dish. Combine yogurt, basil, cornstarch, salt, and pepper and spread over chicken. Mix together breadcrumbs and Parmesan and sprinkle over chicken. Bake at 375° for 30 – 35 minutes until chicken is cooked through.

POTATO CHIP CHICKEN

1 lb. boneless, skinless chicken breasts (2-4 half breasts)
5 T butter
1½ C crushed potato chips
½ tsp freshly ground black pepper
½ tsp crushed rosemary
½ tsp crushed thyme

Melt butter in a 7X11" baking pan and let cool. Mix together crushed potato chips, pepper, rosemary, and thyme in a zip top plastic bag. Dry chicken breasts with a paper towel and roll in melted butter. Drop each piece of buttered chicken into crushed chip mixture in bag and gently press onto breast to completely coat and place in baking pan. Do not crowd chicken pieces. Bake at 375⁰ for 30 minutes or until juices run clear when pierced with a knife.

CHICKEN AND ASPARAGUS BAKE

3 C chicken, cooked and cubed
½ lb. asparagus, lightly steamed
1 can condensed cream soup, undiluted (chicken, mushroom, or celery)
½ C mayonnaise
½ C milk
1 tsp lemon juice
1½ C shredded cheddar or Swiss cheese
½ C crushed butter crackers or croutons
Sprinkle cubed chicken over bottom of a greased 9X13" pan. Evenly place asparagus over top of chicken. Combine soup, mayonnaise, milk, and lemon juice and pour over chicken and asparagus. Sprinkle cheese evenly over all and top with crumbs. Bake at 350° for 30 minutes until golden brown and heated through.

TERIYAKI CHICKEN

2 T teriyaki sauce
2 T brown sugar
2 T minced green onions
1 T lemon juice
4 chicken breast halves
Place first four ingredients into a 1-quart zip top plastic bag. Add chicken breast halves, seal, and marinate in refrigerator for 1 – 2 hours. Remove chicken from marinade, reserving marinade for basting chicken. Place chicken breasts on broiler rack or barbeque grill. Broil 5-6 inches from heat source for 12 – 15 minutes or until done. Brush once or twice with marinade, then discard marinade. Turn once while cooking. Serves 4. This can also be used for pork chops or fish – very good!

DAD'S SWEET AND SOUR SAUCE FOR CHICKEN

1 T sugar

1 T cornstarch

1 T vinegar

1/3 C soy sauce

2/3 C water

1 - 2 lbs. chicken breasts or thighs

Stir together first five ingredients in a small heavy saucepan and cook, stirring constantly, over medium heat, until thickened and clear. Cool. Place chicken on a lightly greased baking pan and brush with cooled mixture. Bake at 350° for 30 minutes to 1 hour, until juices run clear. (Longer time for bone in.) This is very good cooked on a grill and also when used on pork chops.

ORANGE CHICKEN

Place one serving* of chicken on a square of heavy-duty aluminum foil. Add 1 T frozen, defrosted, concentrated, undiluted orange juice and 1 T butter. Salt and pepper, if desired, fold foil, and seal. Bake at 325° for 20 – 25 minutes for boneless or 40-45 minutes for bone in chicken. You may make as many packages as needed to serve. After chicken has baked, if desired, strain juices into a saucepan and add a little cornstarch mixed with cold water. Cook, stirring, over medium heat until thick, to use as a sauce for chicken. This is great served with white or fried rice. *One chicken breast or a leg and a thigh will make one serving.

CHICKEN PARMESAN WITH HERB TOMATO SAUCE

1 - 1½ lbs. boneless, skinless chicken tenders (can use boneless, skinless chicken breast cut in 1" strips and pounded to ½", but chicken tenders are much better).

¾ - 1 C flour in zip-top plastic bag

1 egg, beaten with 2 T water in shallow bowl

In 1-gallon plastic zip-top bag, combine:

1½ C cracker crumbs

½ C grated Parmesan cheese

1 tsp salt

1 tsp freshly ground black pepper

½ tsp each dried thyme leaves, dill weed, marjoram, rosemary, and oregano leaves

Heat ½" olive oil in large skillet over medium to medium-high heat. Dredge chicken pieces in flour, then dip in egg wash and drop into crumb mixture in bag and coat generously with crumbs. Fry in hot oil for approximately 3 minutes on each side until golden brown. Drain on paper towels.

FOR HERB TOMATO SAUCE:

In large pot, sauté 6 large cloves of garlic, minced or pressed, in 3 T olive oil just until aromatic. Spoon one 6 oz. can of tomato paste by tablespoon into hot oil and sauté for 2 - 3 minutes longer, stirring so it doesn't scorch. Add 1- 28 oz. can crushed tomatoes in puree and 1- 14 oz. can chicken broth. To this mixture, add 2 bay leaves, 1 T sugar, 1 tsp each salt and freshly ground black pepper, 1 tsp chili powder, 2 T basil leaves, ½ tsp oregano leaves, 2 T parsley, and ¼ tsp white pepper or cayenne. Simmer for at least 30 minutes for the flavors to blend, or longer for a thicker sauce. Serve hot tenders over cooked Vermicelli topped first with fresh mozzarella and then with heated herb tomato sauce. Sprinkle with additional freshly grated Parmesan if desired.

BOURBON CHICKEN

1½ lb. dark chicken meat, cut into bite size pieces
3 T brown sugar
2 T teriyaki sauce
1 T white sugar
½ tsp Worcestershire sauce
1 C white grape juice
½ tsp garlic salt
½ C bourbon
½ tsp ginger powder
¼ C water

Mix together teriyaki, Worcestershire, garlic salt, ginger, brown sugar, ½ C grape juice, and bourbon. Stir until well blended. Pour 1/3 of sauce over chicken (in a plastic zip top bag). Mix and marinate in the refrigerator for at least three hours (better overnight). Chill remaining sauce. Heat a large skillet over medium heat and cook chicken in its marinade until chicken is done, for three to five minutes. Remove chicken from pan and set aside. Heat remainder of bourbon sauce in this pan and add ½ C white grape juice, 1 T white sugar, and ¼ C water. Bring up to a boil, reduce heat and stir until sugar is dissolved. Add chicken to sauce and stir until coated. This is good over herbed rice or cooked egg noodles.

CHEESY BAKED HERB CHICKEN

1 egg, beaten
½ tsp dried oregano leaves
1 T milk
½ tsp dried marjoram leaves
½ C freshly grated Parmesan cheese
½ tsp dried basil leaves
¼ C cracker crumbs
¼ tsp crushed rosemary
1 T flour
¼ tsp dried sage leaves
1 tsp paprika
Salt and pepper to taste

Beat egg in shallow dish, stir in milk. In another shallow dish, mix together cracker crumbs, flour, Parmesan and all herbs except paprika. Butter or non-stick spray an 8X8" baking pan. Dip chicken breasts in egg mixture, then roll in crumb/cheese mixture. Arrange chicken in pan, sides not touching; sprinkle with paprika. Bake in a preheated 350° oven for 30 minutes, or until juices run clear and chicken is done.

EASY CREAMY CROCKPOT CHICKEN

1 medium onion, diced and sautéed in 2 T butter
1 pkg. dry Italian dressing mix
1 can cream of chicken soup, undiluted
1 cube (1/2 C) butter
¾ C cream cheese, cubed
4 raw chicken breasts, cubed

Combine dressing mix, chicken, onions, and butter in a crockpot. Cook for 4 hours on high or 6 hours on low. ½ hour before serving, add cubed cream cheese and cream of chicken soup and turn up to high. Stir gently once or twice before serving. Spoon over hot biscuits, noodles, mashed potatoes, or rice to serve.

EASY BAR-B-QUE CHICKEN WINGS
1½ lbs. chicken wings
½ C catsup
1½ T Worcestershire sauce
½ tsp prepared yellow mustard
3 T honey
1/3 C lime juice
2 cloves garlic, minced
1 T dried parsley flakes
1 T soy sauce
1 T liquid smoke
½ C water
1 T cornstarch
1 tsp celery salt
1 tsp freshly ground black pepper
1 tsp Tabasco, or to taste
1 T onion powder, if desired

Trim tips from wings and discard. Cut in half for drummies. Prepare a 9X13X2" baking pan or a jellyroll pan by covering with foil (for easy cleanup) and lightly spraying with non-stick spray. Place wings and drummies in a single layer in pan and preheat oven to 350°. Combine all remaining ingredients and whisk together in a small bowl until smooth. Pour over chicken pieces and bake for 1½ hours until chicken is tender. Serves 2 as part of a complete meal. This can easily be doubled.

EASY CHICKEN DIVAN
3 C cubed cooked chicken
½ tsp salt
1 - 10 oz. pkg. frozen broccoli florets, thawed
¼ tsp black pepper
2 - 10 ¾ oz. cans condensed cream of chicken soup, undiluted
1/3 C mayonnaise (not reduced or fat free)
¼ C milk
2 C (8 oz.) shredded taco or Mexican blend or cheddar cheese, divided

In a greased shallow 2½ qt. baking dish, combine the chicken, salt and pepper. Top with the broccoli florets. In a bowl, combine the soup, mayonnaise, milk, and 1½ C shredded cheese. Pour over broccoli and sprinkle with remaining cheese. Bake uncovered, at 375° for 20-25 minutes or until heated through. Submitted by Pat Lewis.

SHREDDED CHICKEN STUFFED CROISSANTS

1 whole chicken breast (can use 4 thighs)
Water or broth, for boiling
Salt and pepper, to taste
½ of an 8 oz. pkg. cream cheese at room temperature
2 T mayonnaise (chipotle flavored, opt.)
½ tsp garlic powder
¼ C chopped green onion
¼ C chopped celery
1 tsp dried parsley
1- 8 count pkg. croissant dough

Cover chicken with water or broth and bring to a boil. Reduce heat and simmer until chicken is very tender, approximately 30 minutes. Drain, cool, and shred, using two forks. Combine cream cheese with mayonnaise, parsley, and garlic powder, season as desired, and add celery and green onion. Gently stir in shredded chicken, adjust mayonnaise if too dry, and chill. Open package of croissants and separate into 4 pieces, pressing sections together to close seam and flattening each to about 4½ - 5" across. Spoon 2 - 3 T filling onto dough. Fold dough up and around filling, pinching together to enclose filling. Place, seam side down, on ungreased baking sheet and bake as directed on croissant package. Use any remaining filling as a sandwich spread, dip for crackers, or to fill more croissants, for company. Chill leftovers.

RITZ CRACKER CHICKEN TENDERS

1 sleeve Ritz crackers, crushed
Salt and pepper, to taste
2 T dry parsley flakes
1 pkg. boneless, skinless chicken tenders
2 T garlic powder
½ C butter, melted

Combine cracker crumbs, salt, pepper, parsley, and garlic powder and place in a shallow dish. Rinse and pat dry chicken tenders, then dip them into the melted butter and roll them in the crumb mixture. Place prepared chicken in a buttered baking dish. Sprinkle any remaining crumbs over chicken and top with any remaining butter. Bake at 350° for 35 minutes or until juices run clear and chicken is crisp and golden.

PERFECTLY ROASTED CHICKEN, ETC.

1 3 – 6 lb. whole chicken, gizzards removed and discarded (or saved for other use), rinsed and patted dry, both inside and out
2 T each, softened butter and olive oil
Freshly ground sea salt and black pepper, to taste
1 tsp each, smoked paprika, rosemary, thyme, sage, celery seed, and parsley (dry herbs)

Lightly oil a 10" Dutch oven (without the lid) or a heavy ovenproof skillet and place in regular or convection oven. Heat oven to 450° and bake empty pot for at least 20 minutes. In a dinner plate, measure and mix together salt, pepper, and herbs. Mix in butter and oil. While pot is heating, ready a couple of paper towels to wipe your hands and set prepared chicken on plate with herb mixture. With your hands, rub herb mixture all over chicken, both inside and out. Tuck wings under chicken. Clean your hands. If you have butcher's string, tie the legs together. When pot is hot, very carefully use hot pads to set hot pot onto stovetop burner or heat proof pad, and using tongs and a spatula, set whole chicken, breast up, into hot pot and return to 450° oven. Roast for 30-35 minutes for 3 - 4 lb. or 45 - 50 minutes for 5 - 6 lb. chicken (to approx. 120-125°). Leave in oven for additional 40 - 45 minutes (temp will continue to rise to 165° - 170°.) Remove from oven and set chicken onto serving plate. Let rest, uncovered, for 15 minutes before slicing and serving. The hot pot will give your dark thigh and leg meat a head start on cooking and along with the chicken breast, will finish flavorful and juicy!

To make both pan broth and gravy, add 1 – 2 C water to juices in pan and cook over medium heat until it comes to a boil, stirring up any bits from the bottom. Reduce heat to a simmer. If desired, separate and remove some of the fat before proceeding or refrigerate for much easier fat separation. Once chilled, fat will just lift off.

To continue for gravy, stir 2-3 T of flour into ½ - ¾ C cool water in a small bowl and whisk well. Pour slowly (through a strainer, if desired) into hot mixture while whisking constantly (you may not use all or may want more, depending on the amount of water used and thickness desired) and cook for at least 5 minutes, until gravy has thickened and raw flour taste is cooked out. Adjust seasoning, if desired.

For the best soup broth, when your meal is complete, remove any remaining meat from carcass and set aside in sealed container in refrigerator to make soup later. Roast carcass, along with any remaining skin and bones, and gizzards and neck if desired, (but not the liver, it's not that great in soup), along with 1 large onion, 2 or 3 garlic cloves, 2 carrots, and 2 celery stalks, quartered, (vegetables-optional) on a rimmed cookie sheet at 450° for 30 minutes, then put them into a crockpot with 2 bay leaves and add water, to cover. Cook overnight on low. Strain and remove bones and solids, then chill to separate fat. Add pan broth and continue for soup. Reserve 1 T of separated fat for noodles.

To make spaetzle-type egg noodles: In a medium bowl, mix together 1 C all-purpose flour, ¼ tsp baking powder, 1 tsp parsley, and a dash of salt. With a fork, mix in 1T room temperature chicken fat (or butter). In a small dish, beat 1 egg with 2 T chicken broth (or milk). Mix together with fork, then knead by hand on a lightly floured surface until smooth. Roll out into a rectangle 1/8" thick, using flour as needed to keep from sticking. Let rest for 5 minutes, then roll up into a log. Use a sharp knife to cut ¼" wide noodles and put into a bowl with more flour to rest, stirring with your fingers to separate and flour all noodles. Let dry as you prepare your soup.

For wonderful chicken noodle soup, Bring reserved chicken broth to a low boil, adding water or purchased chicken broth to make up 6 to 8 cups of broth. Add in 1 T dry parsley and additional ½ tsp each rosemary and thyme if desired. Bring up to a full rolling boil and carefully drop in floured noodles, gently stirring to separate. Cook for at another 20 minutes, lowering heat to a moderate simmer. Broth will thicken with addition of floured noodles. Stir in reserved leftover chicken and continue to cook until heated through. If you prefer a vegetable version, when starting chicken broth, add in 1 onion, diced, 2 carrots, & 2 celery stalks, cut into slices, and simmer for additional 20 minutes before proceeding with noodles. Season to taste.

CHICKEN SOUP (OR FOR POT PIE)

½ batch prepared chicken and broth
1 large potato, peeled and cubed
1 large carrot, scrubbed and cut into coins
1 medium onion, peeled and diced
1 large stalk of celery, rinsed and sliced
¼ green pepper, diced (opt.)
2 T soy sauce
2 T flour
¼ C cold water
Freshly ground black pepper
1-batch biscuits, for topping (Can bake extras separately, if desired.)
Place chicken broth in a medium pot. Add potatoes and carrots and bring to a boil. Cook for 7 – 10 minutes, then add onion, celery and green pepper, if used. Stir in reserved chicken and cook for additional 5 minutes. In a small measuring cup, mix together soy sauce, cold water and flour. Stir until smooth and add to pot. Bring back up to a boil, stirring gently until thickened. This step can be repeated for thicker soup. Let simmer for 20 minutes. Serve as soup or pour into a casserole and top with biscuits. Bake at 400° for 10 - 15 minutes or until biscuits are a rich golden brown. Serve with a salad for a nice comfort meal.

BISCUITS FOR TOPPING POT PIE
2 C flour
2 tsp baking powder
½ tsp baking soda
¼ C cold butter, cut into small cubes
1 tsp salt
2/3 C buttermilk
Sift flour, salt, baking soda, and baking powder together. Add butter, cutting in with a fork. Add buttermilk to make a soft dough. Knead lightly and pat into a 1/3" thick rectangle. Cut into (squares for ease of placement on pot pie, or) circles and place on ungreased baking sheet and bake at 400° for 10 - 12 minutes until golden brown. (For cheddar/herb biscuits, substitute 1 tsp garlic salt for regular salt and add ½ C shredded cheddar when you cut in butter.) For an extra special touch, brush with melted butter just before baking.

COOKIES & BARS

JESSIE WOMBLE'S PEANUT BUTTER COOKIES

1 box yellow or chocolate cake mix
1 C peanut butter
2 eggs
2 T water
½ C vegetable oil

In a large mixing bowl, lightly beat eggs. Stir in oil and water, then mix in the peanut butter. Add cake mix and beat until smooth. Spoon by tablespoon onto lightly greased baking sheets and bake at 350° for 10 minutes. Submitted by Wendy Brock.

PECAN BUTTER COOKIES

1 C butter, slightly softened
½ - ¾ C powdered sugar
1 T vanilla
1¾ C flour, sifted
¼ tsp salt
1 C very finely chopped pecans

Cream together butter and sugar. Add vanilla, then salt, flour, and nuts. Chill for 30 minutes, then spoon out dough in small balls the size of a large olive and gently roll into rounds. Slightly flatten and bake for 12 to 15 minutes at 350° until light brown. They burn fast so do not over bake. Immediately after removing from the oven, sprinkle with powdered sugar.

CRUNCHY PEANUT BUTTER COOKIES

1¼ C extra crunchy peanut butter
1¼ C packed dark brown sugar
¼ C granulated sugar
½ C butter flavored shortening
2 T butter, softened
1 extra large egg
1 T real vanilla
3 T orange juice (or milk)
1 tsp baking soda
½ tsp salt
1¾ C all purpose flour

In a large mixing bowl, cream together peanut butter, shortening, butter, brown sugar and granulated sugar. Beat in egg, vanilla, and orange juice just until smooth. Combine flour, salt, and baking soda together, then add to creamed mixture and mix just until blended. Roll into 1" balls, chilling dough for 30 minutes if too sticky. Place 2" apart on parchment paper lined or ungreased cookie sheet. Dip a fork into water, then into granulated sugar and flatten cookies slightly with a crisscross pattern, dipping into sugar before pressing each cookie. Bake at 375° for 7 minutes in convection oven or 8 minutes in regular oven until golden. Cool for at least 2 minutes before removing to cooling rack.

A#1 COCOA BROWNIES

1 C (2 sticks) butter
2 C sugar
1 T vanilla extract
4 eggs
¾ C cocoa
1 C all-purpose flour
½ tsp baking powder
½ tsp salt
1 C chopped walnuts or pecans (optional)

Preheat oven to 350°. Butter a 13x9x2" baking pan. Melt butter in a saucepan over medium heat or in a large microwave-safe bowl at medium for 2 to 2½ minutes or until melted. Stir in sugar and vanilla. Add eggs, one at a time, whisking after each addition. Add cocoa; beat until well blended. Add flour, baking powder and salt; beat well. Stir in nuts, if desired. Pour batter into prepared pan and bake for 30 to 35 minutes or until brownies begin to pull away from sides of pan. Cool completely in pan on wire rack and cut into bars. (For extra fudgy brownies, drop pan onto counter from about 6" up after removing from oven, then cool and cut as usual.)

TEXAS BROWNIES

2 C flour
2 C sugar
½ C (1 stick) butter
½ C shortening
1 C strong coffee
¼ C cocoa
½ C buttermilk
2 eggs
1 tsp baking soda
1 tsp vanilla

In large bowl, combine flour and sugar. In heavy saucepan, combine butter, shortening, coffee (or water), and cocoa. Stir and heat to boiling and pour boiling mixture over flour and sugar in bowl, mixing well with a wooden spoon. Whisk in buttermilk, eggs, soda, and vanilla until thoroughly blended. Pour into a well-buttered 10x15x1" jellyroll pan. Bake in preheated 400⁰ oven for 20 minutes. While brownies are baking, make frosting:

½ C butter
2 T cocoa
¼ C milk
3½ C powdered sugar
1 tsp vanilla

In saucepan combine butter, cocoa, and milk. Stir and heat to boiling. Remove from heat and stir in powdered sugar and vanilla until frosting is smooth. Pour and spread over brownies as soon as you take them out of the oven. Cool before cutting into squares.

HIP PADDER BARS

1 can sweetened condensed milk
2 T butter
1 – 6 oz. pkg. (1 C) semi-sweet chocolate chips
1 tsp vanilla
½ C (1 cube) butter
1 C firmly packed dark brown sugar
1 egg
1¼ C flour
½ C quick cooking oats
1 C chopped nuts

Combine sweetened condensed milk, 2 T butter, and chocolate chips in heat resistant bowl and microwave on high for 30-45 seconds, then stir, adding 30 seconds more at a time, as needed, to melt chocolate. Stir in vanilla and set aside to cool. Cream together ½ C butter and brown sugar, add egg, and beat until light and fluffy. Mix in flour, oats, and nuts. Pat 2/3 mixture into bottom of lightly buttered 9X13X2" pan. Spread chocolate mixture over oat mixture and spoon remaining oat mixture in small dollops evenly over chocolate filling. Bake at 350⁰ for 25 to 30 minutes, until done. Cool before cutting into squares.

PEANUTTY CANDY BARS

4 C quick cooking oats
2/3 C butter, melted
1 C brown sugar, packed
½ C + 2/3 C peanut butter, divided
½ C light corn syrup
1 tsp vanilla
1 – 11 oz. pkg. butterscotch chips
1 C (6 oz.) semi-sweet chocolate chips
1 C salted peanuts, chopped

In a large bowl, combine oats, brown sugar, butter, ½ C peanut butter, corn syrup, and vanilla. Press into a greased 9X13" baking pan. Bake in a pre-heated 350⁰ oven for 12-14 minutes or until mixture is bubbly around the edges. In a microwave safe bowl, melt together the butterscotch and chocolate chips on high for 30 to 45 seconds. Stir until smooth, adding additional time in microwave in 15-second increments only, just until melted. Stir in peanuts and remaining peanut butter. Spread over cooled oat mixture. Chill for one hour before cutting into squares.

CHOCOLATE PEANUT SQUARES

1 C butter
6 - 1 oz. squares semi-sweet chocolate
1 C angel flake coconut
1½ C graham cracker crumbs
½ C unsalted peanuts, chopped
2 - 8 oz. pkgs. cream cheese, at room temperature
1 C sugar
1 tsp vanilla

Microwave ¾ C butter and 2 - 1 oz. squares of chocolate on high for 1 - 2 minutes, until melted, stirring at 30-second intervals. Stir in graham cracker crumbs, coconut, and peanuts. Press onto bottom of 9X13" pan and chill for 30 minutes. Mix together cream cheese, sugar and vanilla until well blended and smooth. Spread evenly over crumb crust and chill for additional 30 minutes. Microwave remaining butter and chocolate together until melted, stirring every 30 seconds and spread over cream cheese layer. Chill and cut into squares. Makes 48 squares.

HEALTHY COOKIES

In large bowl, mix:
1 C whole-wheat flour
¼ C white flour
½ tsp salt
½ tsp ground ginger
½ tsp ground cinnamon
½ tsp ground cloves
1 tsp baking soda
1 C brown sugar, packed
In another bowl, stir together:
¼ C molasses (or cane syrup)
1 egg
½ C melted butter
Add this to dry mixture and stir together. Stir in 1 C old-fashioned rolled oats (quick oats are okay) and mix well. Drop by spoonful onto greased baking sheets 2" apart. Bake at 375° for 8-10 minutes until golden brown

RAISIN SPICE OATMEAL COOKIES

1 C raisins
2 C all purpose flour
½ C applesauce (1 single serving size)
1 C sugar
1 tsp salt
1 tsp baking soda
2 tsp cinnamon
1 C butter flavor shortening
1 tsp cardamom
2 eggs, beaten
¼ tsp each, ginger and allspice
1 tsp vanilla
3 C old-fashioned oats
In a small saucepan, stir together raisins and applesauce. Add just enough water to cover and simmer until raisins are plumped. Drain raisins, reserving 9 T liquid. Add baking soda and shortening to hot raisin liquid. Cool. Add beaten eggs, vanilla and sifted dry ingredients. Blend until combined, then stir in oats and raisins. Drop by large spoonfuls onto greased or parchment

paper lined baking sheets and bake at 350° for 12-15 minutes, until edges are browning and cookies are set. These cookies do not spread out, so gently press down before baking. They are cake like but cookie easy to eat.

HAYSTACKS (NO-BAKE COOKIES)

2 C sugar
½ C milk
½ C (1 cube) butter
4 T unsweetened baking cocoa
¾ C crunchy peanut butter
½ C sweetened angel flake coconut
3 C quick cooking oats

In a large pot, add sugar, butter, milk, and cocoa. Bring to a boil over medium heat, stirring as it heats. When it comes to a full rolling bowl, cook at a rolling boil for one full minute, without stirring, and remove from heat. Stir in peanut butter, and then stir in oats and coconut. Quickly spoon out onto waxed paper, using 2 spoons to dip in and push off mixture before it sets up or crystalizes. Let cool completely and store in airtight container.

SCOTCHEROOS (NO-BAKE COOKIES)

1 C sugar
1 C white corn syrup
1 C peanut butter (smooth or crunchy)
6 C crisp rice cereal
1 C semisweet chocolate chips
1 C butterscotch chips

Place crisp rice cereal in large mixing bowl. In a heavy saucepan, bring corn syrup and sugar to a boil. Remove from heat and stir in peanut butter until well mixed. Pour over cereal and mix together. Place mixture into a buttered 9X13" pan and gently pat down. Melt chocolate chips and butterscotch chips together and spread over cereal mixture. When firm, cut into squares. Submitted by Nancy Benjamin.

TUMBLEWEEDS (NO BAKE COOKIES)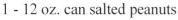

1 - 12 oz. can salted peanuts
3 C butterscotch chips
1 – 7 oz. can potato sticks
3 T peanut butter

Combine peanuts and potato sticks in a bowl and set aside. Heat peanut butter and butterscotch chips in a microwave safe bowl at 70% power in the microwave for 1 – 2 minutes, or until melted, stirring every 30 seconds. Add to peanut mixture. Stir to coat evenly and drop by tablespoon onto waxed paper to harden.

CASHEW MELTS (COOKIES)

1 C butter, at room temperature
½ C powdered sugar
1 tsp vanilla
2 C all purpose flour
Scant 1/8 tsp salt
2 C finely chopped (nearly ground) salted cashews
1½ C powdered sugar, for rolling

Cream together butter and ½ C powdered sugar. Add vanilla. Combine flour, salt, and nuts and add to butter mixture. Stir until it holds together and roll into 1" balls. Place on ungreased cookie sheets (can be close together, they do not spread) and bake in preheated 350° oven for 15 minutes, until lightly browned. While still hot, roll in powdered sugar, and then set on another cookie sheet to cool. When cool, roll again in powdered sugar. These will melt in your mouth!

RASPBERRY MAGIC BARS

½ C melted butter
1½ C graham cracker crumbs
1 – 14 oz. can sweetened condensed milk
1 C angel flake coconut
1 – 12 oz. pkg. semi-sweet chocolate morsels
1 C chopped walnuts
½ C seedless red raspberry jam

Combine melted butter and graham cracker crumbs and press into a 9"X13" baking pan. Pour sweetened condensed milk over crumb mixture. Sprinkle with chocolate morsels, coconut, and chopped nuts. Press down firmly. Warm jam in a small microwave safe bowl on high for 25 to 30 seconds. Stir and drizzle evenly over mixture. Bake at 350° for 25 to 30 minutes until golden brown. Cool completely and cut into bars.

LEMON BARS

Crust:
1 C flour
1/3 C butter, softened
1/3 C powdered sugar
Topping:
1 C granulated sugar
½ tsp lemon extract, optional, ½ tsp vanilla can be substituted
2 eggs, lightly beaten
½ tsp baking powder
3 T flour
¼ tsp salt
¼ C fresh lemon juice
1 tsp grated lemon zest, or more for a tangier flavor
powdered sugar
Combine crust ingredients and pat into an 8" square or 7X11" baking pan. Bake at 375° for 15 minutes. Cool. Meanwhile, combine granulated sugar, eggs, flour, lemon juice, extract, zest, baking powder and salt and mix until frothy. Pour over cooled crust. Bake at 375° for 18 - 22 minutes, until a light golden brown. Sprinkle with powdered sugar when cool and cut into squares.

STRAWBERRY SQUARES

½ C butter, softened
1 tsp baking powder
1 C brown sugar, packed
1 C oats, quick or old fashioned
½ tsp each - almond extract and real vanilla
1 C all purpose flour
dash of salt
¾ C strawberry preserves

Cream together butter and brown sugar until smooth and fluffy. Add almond extract and vanilla. Mix in dry ingredients until combined, but crumbly. Reserve ¼ mixture for topping, and press the rest into a lightly greased 8X8" baking pan. Spoon preserves on top, spreading carefully, then sprinkle with remaining topping. Bake in a preheated 350° regular or convection oven for 30-40 minutes until lightly browned. Cool and then cut into squares to serve.

NUT GOODY BARS

1 C (6 oz.) semisweet chocolate chips
½ C butter
1 C (6 oz.) butterscotch chips
½ bag mini marshmallows
¾ C creamy peanut butter
8 oz. Spanish peanuts

Melt together chocolate and butterscotch chips, butter, and peanut butter. Remove from heat and stir in nuts and marshmallows and quickly spoon into a well-buttered 8 or 9" square pan. Chill and cut into small squares.

ALMOND MACAROONS

1½ C whole blanched almonds
butter or non-stick spray
1 C Splenda Measure (no calorie sweetener)
2 large egg whites
¼ tsp salt
¼ tsp vanilla

In a food processor, finely grind the whole almonds; add Splenda and salt.

In a mixing bowl, beat egg whites until foamy (just before soft peaks form); add vanilla and gently fold into almond mixture. Line a baking sheet with parchment paper and butter or spray with non-stick spray. Spoon batter onto parchment by ½ teaspoonfuls. Bake in the middle of a preheated 300° oven for 20 minutes until golden edged. Cool on parchment paper. Peel off of parchment when cool and store in an airtight container. Note: You can use powdered egg whites, found in the baking aisle of many markets. This is an "Atkins" diet acceptable food. Submitted by Janet Wilder.

COCONUT MERINGUES

2 egg whites, at room temperature
dash salt
½ tsp vanilla
2/3 C sugar
1 – 3½ oz. can flaked coconut

Beat egg whites with dash salt and vanilla until you have soft peaks. Gradually add sugar and continue to beat to stiff peak. Very gently fold in coconut. Drop by tablespoon onto greased or parchment covered cookie sheet and bake in preheated 325° oven for 20 minutes until lightly golden.

PECAN TASSIES

2 (3 oz.) pkg. cream cheese at room temperature
1 C butter, at room temperature
2 C flour
1 C dark brown sugar, packed
1 egg
1 T soft butter
1 tsp vanilla
dash salt
1 C broken pecans, divided

For cream cheese pastry, cream together cream cheese and butter until blended. Stir in flour until well combined. Cover and chill for 1 hour. In the meanwhile, beat together egg, brown sugar, 1 T butter, vanilla, and salt until smooth. When pastry has chilled, shape into 2" balls and press into and up the sides of the muffin cups (approximately 24 pastries/2 muffin pans). Divide half the pecans among the pastry lined muffin cups, then pour egg mixture over nuts. Top with remaining pecans and bake at 325^0 for 25 minutes, until filling is set. Cool, and then remove from pans.

DIPS

SPINACH DIP

1 loaf round dark rye bread
2 C sour cream
1 package (about ½ C) Knorr Leek Soup (dry mix)
10 oz. package chopped spinach
½ C chopped green onions
1 C mayonnaise
1 tsp dill weed
½ C fresh parsley, chopped
¼ tsp garlic powder

Thaw and squeeze spinach as dry as you can. Mix remaining ingredients and stir in spinach. Chill for at least 4 hours. Prepare bread by slicing off the top of the loaf, about ½ to 1" down from the top. Scoop out the insides and tear that part up into chunks to dip into spread. When ready to serve, fill cavity of bread with dip and arrange chunks around the outside. I usually buy an extra loaf of hard crusty bread to cut or tear up to serve along with the inside of the "bowl" loaf of bread. A good choice for this extra loaf is rye/white swirl. Submitted by Patti Coble.

ARTICHOKE DIP

1- 15 oz. can water packed artichokes, drained
¼ C mayonnaise
¼ C sour cream
3 cloves garlic, minced
¼ C shredded cheddar cheese
¾ C grated Parmesan cheese, divided
¼ tsp freshly ground black pepper
1/8 tsp white pepper
Optional: 1 – 4 oz. can diced green chilies

Combine all ingredients except the Parmesan cheese. Add ½ C of the Parmesan and put into a shallow baking dish (9" glass pie plate). Top with the reserved Parmesan and bake at 350° for 20 minutes, or until hot and bubbly. Serve hot with fresh vegetables and chips to dip with. This is my niece Andrea Vasquez's specialty.

HOT ARTICHOKE AND SPINACH DIP

1 - 8 oz. pkg. cream cheese, softened
¼ C mayonnaise, OR sour cream OR Greek yogurt
½ C freshly grated Parmesan cheese
¼ C freshly grated Romano cheese
2 - 3 cloves garlic, peeled and minced
½ tsp dried basil
Freshly ground sea salt and black pepper, to taste
1 – 14 oz. can artichoke hearts, drained and chopped very fine
1 C frozen chopped spinach, thawed and drained very well
¾ C shredded mozzarella cheese

Butter a medium baking dish and preheat oven to 350° degrees. In a medium bowl, cream together cream cheese and mayonnaise, sour cream, OR Greek yogurt. Stir in Parmesan and Romano cheeses, garlic, basil, sea salt and pepper. Add artichokes and spinach and transfer mixture to baking dish and top with shredded mozzarella. Bake for 25 – 30 minutes, until bubbly and lightly browned. This is easily adaptable to your preferences, or good as is. You can add chives or finely chopped green onions or green peppers and/or chopped red peppers or pimientos for holiday color, a few dashes of Frank's hot sauce for extra zip, or even bacon bits or chopped water chestnuts, etc. Serve with tortilla chips and/or veggies.

CREAMY BLUE CHEESE GARLIC DIP

1 C (low fat, if desired) sour cream
2 cloves garlic, minced
½ C dry nonfat milk powder
2 oz. crumbled blue cheese
1 T grated onion
½ tsp freshly ground black pepper
1 T fresh lemon juice
½ tsp salt
1 tsp dry parsley flakes
1 T diced chives or green onion, tops only (opt.)

Combine and mix until smooth. Chill for 2 hours to blend flavors. Serve with fresh vegetables, chips, or crackers.

CLAM DIP

2 – 3 oz. pkg. cream cheese
½ tsp onion powder
1 – 7 oz. can minced clams
½ tsp Worcestershire sauce
1 T fresh lemon juice
Salt, to taste

Drain liquid from clams and save. Stir to soften cream cheese and mix in clams. Add seasonings and enough reserved clam juice for consistency. Chill for 2 hours and serve with chips.

MY FAVORITE GARLIC RED PEPPER HUMMUS

2 T olive oil
salt, to taste, if desired
juice from 1 lemon
3 – 5 garlic cloves, minced (I go for more!)
¼ C Tahini (sesame butter)
½ - 1 tsp Mrs. Dash Garlic & Herb
3 – 4 shakes of garlic Tabasco sauce (or regular Tabasco sauce, to taste-it's hotter)
1 – 2 roasted red peppers (roasted fresh, or from a jar)
1 – 17 oz. jar or 15 oz. can garbanzo beans, drained- save liquid

In a food processor, combine oil, lemon juice, garlic, and tahini. Process until smooth. Add garbanzo beans and seasonings and process until creamy, thinning with saved bean liquid to desired consistency. Add chunks of roasted red peppers to processor and tap processor to barely chop. Turn out into bowl and stir with a spoon to distribute peppers evenly. Chill for 2 – 3 hours for flavors to meld. Great with veggies, whole grain crackers, or pita bread triangles. This is also good as a filling for pita sandwiches, along with sprouts and/or some of your other favorite crunchies.

APRICOT FRUIT DIP

1-10 oz. jar apricot-pineapple preserves
1 tsp creamy horseradish
1½ tsp dry mustard
1/8 tsp crushed red pepper
1- 8 oz. pkg. cream cheese, at room temperature
½ C chopped roasted peanuts

Beat together the first five ingredients and chill for 30 minutes. Set out for 10 minutes, then top with chopped nuts and serve with fresh sliced bananas, apples and peaches. My niece Andrea Vasquez served this at a family dinner party and was it ever a hit. It is wonderfully tangy and refreshing.

PICO DE GALLO

2 medium jalapeños
1 Hungarian yellow pepper
½ medium sweet green pepper
1 Serrano or habanero chili, optional
1 large red or white onion, cut into quarters
3 garlic cloves
juice of 2 limes
1 T olive oil, optional but good
8 Italian plum tomatoes, diced small
1½ C packed fresh cilantro leaves, chopped
freshly ground black pepper and sea salt, to taste

Using kitchen gloves, rinse and quarter all of the peppers, removing seeds and white inner ribs (can leave some if you like it hot!). Peel the garlic cloves and rinse the limes and slice in half. If you have a food processor, now is the time to use it. Place pepper pieces, garlic cloves, and lime juice in processor and pulse quickly 5 or 6 times to roughly mince, but not juice, the peppers. You may do this in smaller amounts if you only have a small processor, or you can finely dice or mince if you don't have a processor at all. Do NOT over process! Remove to a plastic or glass bowl and do the same with your onion. Add to your peppers and garlic. Finely dice your tomatoes and chop your cilantro (not in processor) and add to your pepper mixture. Add the olive oil and salt and pepper to taste. Serve with black beans, chips, tacos, etc. Cover and chill leftovers. Keeps for several days in the refrigerator.

GUACAMOLE

3 Haas avocados, peeled and pitted
2 garlic cloves, minced or pressed
Juice of 2 limes
1 tsp chipotle powder or 2 tsp chili powder
1 tsp sea salt
½ tsp freshly cracked black pepper
¼ C freshly chopped cilantro

Mash together avocado and lime juice. Stir in minced garlic, chipotle powder, salt, pepper, and cilantro. Taste and adjust seasonings, if desired. I have also been known to add in a couple of tablespoons of fresh Pico de Gallo for a change of pace.

FISH & SEAFOOD

SCALLOPED OYSTERS

1½ qt. oysters and their liquid
salt & freshly ground black pepper
2½ C cracker crumbs
1 T Worcestershire sauce
¾ C melted butter
2 T dry sherry
¾ C light cream

In a 2 qt. baking dish, layer oysters, crumbs, liquid from oysters, butter, salt and pepper. Mix together cream, Worcestershire sauce, and sherry. Pour over all and bake in a preheated 350° oven for 25 – 30 minutes or until oysters begin to curl.

CAJUN SHRIMP

2 lbs. uncooked peeled large shrimp
¼ C butter
1 tsp freshly ground pepper
¼ C olive oil
1 T Worcestershire sauce
½ tsp salt
Juice of one lemon
1 tsp cayenne pepper

Heat oven to 400°. Combine all but shrimp in wide ovenproof skillet big enough to hold shrimp in one layer. Place skillet in oven just long enough to melt butter. Add shrimp and stir to coat. Bake 10 - 15 minutes, stirring occasionally. Remove from oven just as they turn pink- they will cook another minute or two in hot skillet. The shrimp makes a lot of juice for a dipping sauce or for pouring over hot rice, noodles, or garlic toast.

SCAMPI-STYLE SHRIMP

½ - ¾ lb. raw, shelled & deveined shrimp (31-40 Count)
6 T butter
½ tsp salt
1 T olive oil
1 tsp dried basil leaves or 2 T fresh, minced
2 T sliced green onions
1 tsp dried parsley leaves or 2 T fresh, minced
6 large cloves garlic, minced or pressed
½ tsp Tabasco, or more to taste
½ tsp freshly ground pepper
3 oz. Parmesan cheese, from block, freshly grated

Preheat oven to broil. Heat wide, oven-safe skillet over medium high heat. Pour olive oil, then butter into skillet and quickly add green onions, garlic, basil, parsley, salt, pepper, and Tabasco. As herbs become aromatic, watching carefully so as not to burn, quickly stir in shrimp, raising heat to high. Sauté quickly until shrimp is just turning pink. Remove from heat and place under broiler for one to two minutes. Remove from oven and top with grated Parmesan. Place back under broiler just long enough to start to melt Parmesan to a golden brown. Great served with rice pilaf and fresh steamed asparagus.

SHRIMP IN BACON

1 lb. cleaned and shelled raw shrimp
6 slices of bacon, diced
4 tsp lemon juice
1 clove of garlic, minced
1 T chopped parsley

Fry bacon until crisp. Drain on paper towels. Add shrimp to hot grease in pan and stir until shrimp turns pink. Quickly add garlic, parsley, and lemon juice. Cook together for two to three minutes. Serve immediately over steamed herb rice or cheese grits.

SZECHWAN STYLE SHRIMP***

8 T water
1 T rice vinegar
4 T tomato paste* (or ketchup, it IS ok!)
1 T lime juice
½ tsp ground ginger
2 T soy sauce
2 T cornstarch
1 T honey
1 tsp dried cilantro leaves
½ tsp crushed red chili peppers (to taste)
6 cloves garlic, minced
½ C sliced green onions
1 lb. (16 - 25 to a pound) peeled raw shrimp (fresh or frozen, defrosted)
3 T vegetable oil
2 - 3 T Toasted sesame seeds, optional

In a medium bowl, combine water, tomato paste or ketchup, soy sauce, cornstarch, honey, rice vinegar, lime juice, crushed red pepper, cilantro, and ginger. Set aside. Heat oil in a large skillet over medium high heat. Stir in green onions and garlic. Cook for 1 minute, then stir in shrimp and sauté just until shrimp begins to pink and become opaque. Stir in combined liquid mixture and gently stir and cook until sauce has thickened and is bubbly. Do not overcook, as the shrimp will become rubbery. This only takes a short time to cook and is wonderful over steamed Jasmine rice. Note** 1 - 1 ½ Cups of lightly steamed broccoli, snow peas, and/or sliced red peppers and water chestnuts make a good addition, sautéed and then added just before serving. Top with toasted sesame seeds, if desired. ***Don't let the list of ingredients fool or intimidate you. This is such a simple dish to prepare. Nick loves this, without the onions, of course, and it is so good, just as is. I like broccoli and water chestnuts for crunch, but it's not hard to spoon Nick's out, and then add the heated veggies to mine. *Spoon extra tomato paste onto wax paper coated plate by tablespoonful, freeze, then wrap individual tablespoonfuls in plastic and store, frozen, in airtight zip top plastic bag for later use.

SHRIMP HORS D'OEUVRES

1 lb. Bay shrimp, cooked, chilled
1-2 ripe avocados, diced
½ C chopped tomatoes
½ C red onion, chopped
½ C catsup
¼ C lime juice
¼ C fresh cilantro, chopped
Hot pepper sauce, to taste

Combine all ingredients together gently and chill for 2 – 3 hours to blend flavors. Serve with crackers or chips. Submitted by Marilyn Blintz.

SHRIMP CREOLE

3 C peeled shrimp
4 T bacon drippings (or 3T olive oil & 1 T butter)
3 large cloves of garlic, minced
1 C green pepper, diced
1½ C celery, diced
2 – 15 oz. cans crushed tomatoes in juice
3 T tomato paste
1 T chili powder
1 tsp each freshly ground pepper and sea salt
½ tsp crushed thyme leaves
½ tsp crumbled oregano leaves
1 tsp hot pepper (Tabasco) sauce

Sauté garlic in drippings until aromatic. Add onions, peppers, and celery to skillet and cook to crisp, tender. Stir in tomatoes and tomato paste, add salt, pepper, thyme, oregano, chili, and hot sauce and simmer for 10 minutes. Add shrimp and gently simmer for 15 minutes more, until shrimp is pink and translucent. Serve over steamed rice. Serves 6.

BASIL BROILED SALMON

2 - 4 to 6 oz. salmon steaks
3 T olive oil
1 garlic clove, minced
2 T fresh lemon juice
1 C fresh basil leaves
½ C freshly grated Parmesan cheese
2 tsp Dijon mustard
1/8 tsp cayenne or chipotle pepper, optional

Combine olive oil, garlic, and lemon juice in small food processor. Process in 2 or 3 short bursts. Add basil, Parmesan and mustard. Process, in 2 or 3 bursts, just long enough to blend well. Preheat oven for broiling. Put one-fourth of basil sauce in bottom of 9-inch oven-safe dish. Arrange salmon on top of sauce and spoon remaining sauce over top of salmon. Sprinkle with cayenne or chipotle pepper, if used. Broil in preheated oven for 16 to 20 minutes or until fish flakes easily when tested with a fork.

SCALLOP STIR FRY WITH CASHEWS

8 – 10 oz. fresh or thawed frozen scallops
1 medium white onion, sliced thinly
1 large stalk celery, sliced diagonally
3 or 4 large mushrooms, sliced
1 baby eggplant, cut in ½ and sliced
½ C fresh broccoli florets
1 – 8 oz. can sliced water chestnuts, drained
4 cloves garlic, peeled and minced
¼ to ½ tsp crushed red pepper (to taste)
4 T soy sauce
1 tsp garlic bean sauce (opt)
3 T olive oil
½ C salted cashew halves
steamed rice

Heat a large skillet on medium high until hot. Add olive oil to skillet and quickly dump in prepared vegetables and garlic. Stir-fry until crisp tender only, then add scallops and crushed peppers, continuing to stir-fry. Add soy and bean sauce, if used. Cook for 2 to 3 minutes and stir in cashews. Remove from heat and serve with or over steamed rice.

SIMPLE BATTER FRIED FISH

½ lb. fresh or frozen cod fillets

2 T flour plus extra for dredging

¼ tsp each of garlic powder, onion powder, salt, cayenne, and paprika

1/8 tsp each of dried crushed thyme and oregano

1/3 C club soda (or beer)

Oil for frying

Rinse fillets in cold water and pat dry, then dredge in flour. In shallow bowl, combine 2 T flour, seasonings, and club soda. Heat 1 inch of oil to 365° in a heavy skillet. Dip floured fillets in batter and fry 2 or 3 at a time in hot oil for 2-3 minutes until done. Drain on paper towels and serve hot.

SIMPLE PAN FRIED FISH

1   4 – 6 oz. fish filet per person (cod, halibut, perch, tilapia, snapper, or other firm fish)

½ to 1 C all purpose flour, for dusting fish

Freshly ground sea salt and black pepper, to taste

¼ - ½ tsp onion or garlic powder, optional

Butter or olive oil for frying

Lemon slices and dried parsley, for garnish**

Heat a large, heavy skillet over medium heat for at least 10 minutes before you are ready to cook. Place flour on a paper plate or pie plate and using a fork, mix in salt and pepper, and onion or garlic powder, if used. Gently lay fish filets, one at a time, in flour and dust flour onto both sides. Gently shake off excess flour. Add your butter or oil to skillet and as soon as it melts and bubbles, set fish into pan. Cook, without turning for at least 3 minutes, or until browned. Using a flexible spatula, gently turn fish and brown remaining side. Depending on the thickness of your filets, this may be enough for your fish to be ready. If fish flakes easily in the thickest part, it is done. If not, cook for a couple more minutes, lowering heat if necessary, until it flakes. **For a light sauce, stir ¼ C fresh lemon juice and/or white wine into pan when fish is done and out of the pan. Sprinkle in some dried parsley for a touch of color and flavor. Swirl pan gently to warm and stir up any browned bits and pour over fish. Serve with lemon slices, if desired.

PAN SEARED BLACKENED FISH

2 – ½ - ¾" thick salmon or other firm fish filets, 4-6 oz. each
2 T olive oil
2 T softened butter (mixed with 1 tsp soy sauce or Worcestershire, opt.)
½ tsp each paprika, dried basil, rosemary, sugar, freshly ground sea salt and ground black pepper
1/8 tsp cayenne, or white pepper
Optional: freshly sliced lemon for serving
Combine seasonings in a small bowl. Gently pat fish dry with paper towel. Rub softened butter onto fish and sprinkle seasoning mix over all sides. Heat olive oil in a large skillet over medium high heat to almost smoking. Carefully place filets in skillet and cook for 2-3 minutes or until browned. Use a spatula to turn and then cook until fish begins to flake when fork is inserted and fish has browned and is done to your liking. This method works well for other firm fish, and you can use your favorite purchased spice blend for convenience.

CHESAPEAKE BAY CRAB CAKES

1 lb. crabmeat mix (back fin and claw)
7 saltine crackers, crushed
1 egg, beaten
1 dash of Tabasco hot sauce
1 dash of Worcestershire sauce
1 - 2 T mayonnaise
1 T mustard
1 T Old Bay seasoning
Combine everything but the crabmeat. Gently add in the crabmeat and form into small patties. Chill for 20 minutes. Fry over low heat in ½" to 1" of peanut oil for about 10 minutes per side until golden brown. Submitted by Jean Drummond.

NICK'S CLAM CHOWDER

2 – 10 oz. cans of whole baby clams, or minced clams (your preference)
1 bottle clam juice
32 oz. chicken stock or vegetable broth, divided
3 med Yukon or russet potatoes, peeled and cubed
6 slices bacon or 5 half-slices of salt pork, diced very small
3 cloves garlic, diced very small or minced
¾ C diced celery, with leaves
2 baby carrots, diced very small
2 bay leaves
1 tsp dried thyme leaves, crushed in your palm
1 T Worcestershire sauce
¼ tsp white pepper, or more, to taste
3 T flour
½ C heavy cream
¾ C milk

In a large pot, cook cubed potatoes in 3½ C chicken stock, reserving ½ C stock for later use. Cook over medium heat for approximately 10 minutes or until tender. Add in clam juice, bay leaves, and thyme and turn down to a light simmer. While that is cooking, sauté diced bacon or salt pork in a skillet until very crisp and browned. Drain crispy bits on paper towels and set aside. Add diced celery with leaves and carrots to rendered bacon fat in skillet and cook for 5 – 10 minutes. Add in garlic and cook for another minute or two, then stir in 3 heaping tablespoons of flour. Cook and stir constantly for 5 minutes to thoroughly cook flour. Gently pour in milk and cream, continuing to stir constantly. Add in reserved chicken broth, cooking and stirring for at least 5 minutes until thick and smooth. (You can add broth from soup if too thick.) Remove from heat and stir into potatoes, raising the heat just a bit, continuing to stir until soup has thickened. When carrots are tender, add clams with their juice, and crispy bacon. Season with white pepper and Worcestershire sauce and cook gently for 5 minutes more to heat clams. NOTE***Do NOT add additional salt without tasting! Serve with saltines or oyster crackers. For a special treat, add a drop of truffle oil to each bowl just before serving. Serves 3 or 4 as a meal, more as a side.

MAIN DISHES & CASSEROLES

PEPPER STEAK

1 ½ lb. round steak or London broil, partially frozen
¾ C soy sauce
1 T sugar
¾ tsp ground ginger
3 cloves garlic, minced
3 T olive oil
1 T butter
2 green peppers, seeded and cut into thin strips
2 medium onions, thinly sliced
6 medium Roma tomatoes, cut into eighths
2 T cornstarch
¼ C water
Steamed rice or cooked egg noodles, for serving

Cut meat across the grain into paper-thin slices while partially frozen, for ease in cutting. Place meat in a bowl and stir in soy sauce, sugar, and ground ginger. Marinate, covered, in the refrigerator, stirring occasionally for at least 30 minutes or up to 5 hours. 20 minutes before you are ready to prepare, remove meat from refrigerator and set aside. In a large skillet, over medium heat, sauté minced garlic in olive oil and butter until aromatic. Add peppers and onions and sauté for 3 minutes. Raise heat to high and add in meat with its marinade. Cook, stirring, until meat is cooked through, 3 – 5 minutes. Reduce heat and spoon tomatoes on top; cover and simmer for a few minutes, until tomatoes release their juices. Blend 2 T cornstarch into ¼ C cold water and gently stir into mixture. Cook for another minute or two until slightly thickened. Serve over steamed rice or cooked egg noodles. Serves 6.

CHICKEN CHOW MEIN

1 medium chicken
1 large onion, chopped
2 C celery, thinly sliced at an angle
1 – 15 oz. can fancy Chinese vegetables
1 – 8 oz. can sliced water chestnuts
3 T olive oil
1 T butter
½ tsp each salt and pepper
2 T cornstarch
1 tsp sugar
2 T cold water
¼ C soy sauce
steamed rice, for serving
crispy Chinese noodles, optional, for serving
slivered almonds, optional, for serving

Place chicken in pot with enough water to cover and cook until tender, 45 minutes to 1 hour. Remove chicken from broth and set aside to cool. Strain broth and chill until ready to use. Remove skin and bones from chicken and discard. Shred chicken and set aside. Cook onions and celery in oil and butter until crisp tender. Add drained Chinese vegetables and water chestnuts, chicken and its broth (remove fat if desired), and cook until hot through. Mix together cornstarch, sugar, soy sauce and cold water and stir into chicken and vegetables. Bring up to just boiling and mixture thickens. Cook for 2 to 3 minutes more and serve over steamed rice and/or Chinese noodles. Top with slivered almonds, if desired.

FRIED RICE WITH SHRIMP AND EGGS

¼ C vegetable oil
½ lb. fresh shrimp, shelled, cleaned and diced
1 C long grain rice, uncooked
2 eggs, lightly beaten
1 envelope dry chicken noodle soup mix
¼ tsp black pepper
2½ C boiling water
1½ T soy sauce
2 small green onions, thinly sliced

In medium skillet, heat 2 T oil and sauté rice until golden brown. Combine dry soup mix and boiling water and stir into rice. Cover, reduce heat, and simmer for 30 minutes until liquid is absorbed. In another skillet, heat remaining oil and stir in cut up shrimp. Cook for 1 or 2 minutes and quickly stir in beaten eggs. Add pepper and soy sauce. Stir shrimp and egg mixture into rice mixture until combined. Serve topped with sliced green onions.

OUR FAVORITE CHINESE STYLE CHICKEN FRIED RICE

3 C cold cooked rice*

7 T vegetable oil, divided

2 T toasted sesame oil

¼ C oyster sauce**

3 T Tamari (soy) sauce**

3 drops fish sauce**

Freshly ground spicy pepper mix, to taste or 1 tsp red chili flakes

2 eggs, lightly beaten with 1T water

½ medium zucchini, diced large***

1 large shallot, thinly sliced

3 large mushrooms, sliced

1 broccoli crown, separated into florets

2 – 3 T diced fresh jalapeño, to taste (optional)

2 boneless, skinless chicken breasts, cubed or thinly sliced

Using a very large skillet or wok, heat 1 T oil over medium high heat, using a paper towel to spread the oil over the hot surface, and pour in the beaten egg when oil is hot. Tip the skillet to spread egg over entire surface and when it looks dry (only moments) turn off heat. Use a flat spatula to roll the egg up and turn onto a (paper) plate. Slice with a sharp knife into 1/8" wide spirals. Set aside. Add 2 T oil to skillet and again heat over medium high heat. When oil shimmers, stir in vegetables and sauté just until crisp-tender. Turn out onto plate and set aside. Add 2 T oil to skillet and heat again to a shimmer. Add chicken to skillet and cook chicken, stirring only as necessary until no longer pink. Turn chicken onto plate and set aside. If needed, wipe skillet of any food particles (using a very hot skillet for these steps should leave you with a smooth, oiled surface) and add remaining 2 T vegetable oil. Heat to a shimmer over medium high heat and add in cold rice, stirring to separate grains, but not turn to mush. Add in your three sauces and pepper or chili flakes and gently stir to combine. When rice is hot and beginning to crisp, add in your reserved meat, egg, and vegetables, and continue to stir-fry until all is hot through. Top with sesame oil; give a final stir and serve. I use additional soy sauce, rather than salt if needed and offer toasted sesame seeds for topping, if desired. Spice Hunter offers a great (salt-free) Szechwan Seasoning Blend that includes sesame seeds and complimentary spices that Nick adores! *Make your rice ahead and cool completely on a parchment or non-stick cookie sheet if you have no leftover rice. Warm, wet rice gets mushy and sticks! **These sauces can be found in the Oriental or ethnic food aisle of most grocery stores. ***Vegetable (and meat) amounts can be adjusted to your preference! You can add in others too, such as bean sprouts and sugar pea pods. I use a separate skillet to cook the vegetables and add 1/4 of the rice, chicken, and egg mix, for me. That way, we can both enjoy!

NICK'S CHICKEN RICE SKILLET

2 boneless, skinless chicken breasts, cut into ¾" cubes
1 C flour
½ tsp dried parsley
½ tsp dried rosemary
½ tsp dried thyme
½ tsp dried sage
1 tsp each salt and pepper
½ C butter
3 C cold steamed rice

Combine all of the herbs and spices with the flour in a large zip top bag and drop in chicken pieces, a few at a time, shaking to coat all of the chicken pieces well. Set aside while heating a large skillet over medium high heat. When skillet is hot, add in half of the butter and quickly drop in several flour-coated pieces of chicken, adding chicken and more butter, as needed, to brown chicken. Try not to stir until pieces have time to brown. When all chicken pieces are browned, stir in rice and continue to stir and fry mixture until hot through, chicken is done, and rice begins to brown. Adjust seasonings and serve with a side vegetable. Serves 3 or 4.

RICE AND VERMICELLI

½ C butter, no substitute
5-6 lg. cloves garlic, minced
½ pkg. Vermicelli or angel hair pasta, broken into pieces
1 C long grain rice, uncooked
4 C water
½ tsp powdered garlic
5 chicken bouillon cubes, or 5 tsp chicken bouillon concentrate

Melt butter in a large skillet that has a lid. Sauté the garlic for 1 - 2 minutes. Stir in the rice and pasta pieces and cook until light brown. Pour in the water and stir in the chicken bouillon. Mix everything together and bring to a boil. Lower heat, sprinkle with the powdered garlic, cover and simmer for 20 minutes. This is better made the day before and it freezes well. Submitted by Shirl Good.

PINEAPPLE CHEESE CASSEROLE

1 20 oz. can chunk pineapple
1 C sharp cheddar cheese, grated
½ C sugar
2 T butter
3 T flour
1 roll Ritz crackers, crumbled

Drain pineapple, reserve juice. Combine flour and sugar; mix with juice and stir into pineapple. Add cheese, mix well, and pour into a greased 8X8" baking dish. Melt butter and mix into crushed crackers. Sprinkle over pineapple mixture. Bake at 350° for 30 minutes. This recipe can easily be doubled and baked in a 9X13" pan for potlucks or family gatherings. Submitted by Ev Siranni

PINEAPPLE CASSEROLE

1 – 20 oz. can crushed pineapple
½ C sugar
3 T flour
1 C shredded cheddar cheese
½ C melted butter or margarine
½ C cheese cracker crumbs

Drain crushed pineapple, reserving 3 T pineapple juice. Combine flour and sugar. Stir in reserved pineapple juice. Add cheese and crushed pineapple, mixing well. Spoon mixture into greased one-quart casserole dish. Combine melted butter and cracker crumbs. Sprinkle over pineapple mixture. Bake at 350° for 20 – 30 minutes or until crumbs are lightly browned. Submitted by Carole Williams.

TWICE BAKED POTATO CASSEROLE
6 medium unpeeled potatoes, scrubbed and baked
2 C shredded mozzarella
¼ tsp each salt and pepper
2 C shredded cheddar
1 lb. bacon cooked, drained, and crumbled
3 green onions, sliced (or 3 T fresh chives, chopped)
3 C sour cream (24 oz.)
Cut unpeeled baked potatoes into 1" cubes. Place half of potatoes into 9X13" greased baking pan. Sprinkle with ½ of the salt, pepper, and bacon. Top with ½ of the sour cream and the cheeses. Repeat layers. Bake, uncovered, at 350° for 25-30 minutes until cheese is melted.

HAM AND CHEESE BRUNCH CASSEROLE
1 – 8 oz. loaf French bread, cut into ¾" cubes
8 oz. cooked ham, cut into ½" cubes
1½ C small broccoli florets
2 C (8 oz.) shredded cheddar cheese
6 eggs, beaten
2 T Dijon mustard
2½ C milk
2 T melted butter
Layer ½ of the bread, ½ of the ham, all the broccoli and ½ the cheese in a greased 9X13" pan. Layer the rest of the bread, ham, and cheese, pressing down lightly. (Pan will be full.) In bowl, beat together eggs, mustard, milk, and butter. Pour over mixture in pan. Let stand for 15 minutes or cover and chill overnight. Bake at 350° for 45 – 50 minutes or until golden brown and set.

SAUERKRAUT CASSEROLE

2 cans sliced potatoes, drained
1 large can sauerkraut, drained
1 lb. precooked Kielbasa, sliced
1 C salad dressing
1 can cream of mushroom condensed soup, undiluted
½ C margarine, melted
½ C dry breadcrumbs

Place potatoes in a greased 9X13" baking pan. Top evenly with sauerkraut, then scatter sliced Kielbasa over that. Mix together the salad dressing, condensed soup, and enough water to rinse the can (approximately ½ C). Pour over the meat. Top with breadcrumbs and drizzle with melted margarine. Bake at 350° for 30 minutes. (This can also be layered in the crockpot and cooked on low for 6 - 8 hrs.) Submitted by Diane Ferguson.

BROCCOLI CHEESE CASSEROLE

2 eggs, lightly beaten
½ C mayonnaise
1 can cream of mushroom condensed soup, undiluted
2 C shredded cheddar cheese
3 T dried minced onion, soaked in a little water and drained

Mix above ingredients together, in order, in a large bowl. Add 2 – 10 oz. packages of frozen broccoli that have been thawed and drained and mix together well. Pour into a lightly greased casserole and bake at 350° for one hour or until bubbly and browned on top. Submitted by Anne Cilio.

ZUCCHINI CORN CASSEROLE

1 medium onion, chopped
1 clove garlic, minced
2 T butter
2 medium zucchini cut in half lengthwise and sliced ¼"thick
1 can Mexicali corn
1½ C shredded cheddar cheese

In 2 qt. saucepan, sauté onion and garlic in butter until onion becomes transparent but not browned. Stir in zucchini and steam, covered, for 3 minutes. Remove from heat and mix in drained Mexicali corn and shredded cheddar. Turn into a lightly buttered casserole and bake at 350⁰ for 25 minutes until cheese is melted and vegetables are tender.

WESTERN BEAN CASSEROLE

8 strips of bacon
½ C BBQ sauce
2 large onions, chopped
4 T dark brown sugar
1 lb. ground beef
4 T blackstrap molasses
1 lb. pork sausage
1 tsp chili powder
1 – 15 oz. can red kidney beans
1 tsp soy sauce
1 – 15 oz. can lima beans
salt and pepper, to taste
1 lg. can pork and beans
2 – 4 cloves garlic, diced
½ C catsup

Cut bacon into bite sized pieces; add chopped onions and fry in one pan. In second pan, cook ground beef and sausage until thoroughly browned. Drain both pans and combine with all of the rest of the ingredients in a large casserole dish. Stir well and bake at 350° for 45 to 60 minutes or put in a crockpot for 4 to 6 hours on low. Submitted by Ev Sirianni.

CHEESEBURGER PEPPER CUPS

4 medium sweet peppers, red, yellow, or green (or a combination)
1 T Worcestershire sauce
½ lb. ground beef
1 T spicy mustard
¼ C chopped onion
½ tsp garlic salt
2 C cooked rice
¼ tsp pepper
1 (6oz.) can tomato paste
1 C beef broth
2 T catsup
1 C shredded Cheddar cheese

Cut peppers in half, lengthwise, and seed. Set aside. Cook beef and onion over medium heat until done. Drain. Stir in rice, tomato paste, catsup, Worcestershire, mustard, garlic salt, and pepper. Spoon into peppers. Place in greased 9X13X2" pan. Pour broth around peppers. Cover with aluminum foil and bake at 350° for 30 minutes. Remove foil and sprinkle with grated cheese. Bake uncovered five minutes longer. Serves four.

TATER TOTS AND HAMBURGER HOT DISH

1 lb. ground beef
½ C milk
1 medium onion, chopped
1 C grated cheddar cheese
1 can cream of mushroom condensed soup, undiluted
1 10 oz. pkg. frozen Tater Tots

Brown ground beef and onion in a hot skillet. Drain and add undiluted soup and milk. Mix well. Add the Tater Tots and pour into a 12X9" baking dish. Top with grated cheese and bake in a pre-heated 375° oven for 35 - 45 minutes. Submitted by Sara Wardlow.

BEEF AND NOODLES

1 – 2 to 3 lb. beef rump or arm roast
2 - 15 oz. cans beef broth
2 bay leaves
½ tsp thyme
½ tsp marjoram
1 tsp freshly ground pepper
½ tsp garlic powder
½ tsp onion salt
2 carrots, cleaned and sliced into coins
1 medium onion, cut into large dice
2 ribs of celery, cleaned and sliced ½" thick
½ of a 24 oz. bag Reames frozen noodles

Brown roast in 3 T oil in hot skillet until browned on all surfaces. Transfer to a crockpot. Pour ½ of the broth into slightly cooled skillet and stir up any loose bits of flavor from skillet. Put all of the broth with meat into crockpot and add spices and vegetables. Cook on high for 3 hours or low for 7 hours. Remove meat and cut or shred into bite size pieces, removing any fat or undesired bits. Return to pot and add ½ of a 24 oz. bag of Reames frozen egg noodles straight from the bag. Gently stir together and continue cooking for an additional hour or until noodles are hot and tender and broth has thickened. May need to add a small amount of water or broth to your preference. Serve with salad and biscuits or hot bread if desired. *Cook's notes. Substitute a chicken for the roast, chicken broth for the beef broth, and ground sage for the marjoram for chicken and noodles. Searing the roast adds flavor, but is not necessary. Pre-browning the chicken is not needed at all. Leftovers can be frozen and reheated.

INDIAN TACOS

1 lb. lean ground beef
2 – 15 oz. cans pinto beans
2 T chili powder
3 – 4 oz. cans diced green chilies
2 T cornstarch
½ C cold water
salt and pepper, to taste
Indian fry bread, for serving (recipe in Breads)
shredded lettuce, for serving
shredded cheddar cheese, for serving
diced onions, for serving
diced tomatoes, for serving
sliced jalapeños, for serving
salsa, for serving

Cook ground beef until crumbly and cooked through. Drain. Add undrained beans, chili powder, salt and pepper, and undrained chilies and bring up to a boil. Reduce heat and simmer until heated through. Mix cornstarch and cold water together and stir into meat and bean mixture, cooking until thickened and smooth. Add a small amount of water if too thick. To serve, spoon mixture over individual Indian fry breads and top with shredded cheese and your choice of fixings. Freeze or refrigerate leftovers for another day.

<u>MEATS</u>

HERBED BRAISED PORK CHOPS

3 bone-in pork chops or 2 pair butterfly pork chops, cut 1" thick
Freshly ground sea salt & black pepper, to taste
1 T each olive oil and butter
1 large white onion, thinly sliced
½ tsp each thyme, rosemary, sage, & dill
1 T lemon juice

Season chops with salt and pepper. Heat olive oil and butter in skillet over medium heat. Brown chops on both sides, then set aside. Add onion and herbs to skillet, stirring gently to distribute seasonings. Place chops on top of onions and reduce heat to low. Cover and cook for 15 to 20 minutes, until tender and done to your taste. Remove chops from pan and discard as much fat as possible. Stir in lemon juice. Spoon onion mixture over pork chops to serve.

MARINATED PORK TENDERLOIN ON THE GRILL

2 whole pork tenderloins (usually comes 2 to a package; can prepare 1 and freeze the other separately, or in marinade, thawing later in the refrigerator)

1/3 C soy sauce

1/3 C fresh lime (or lemon) juice

2 T Worcestershire sauce

6 - 8 large cloves of garlic, minced

1/3 C olive oil (I like extra virgin olive oil)

1 tsp thyme leaves

1 tsp basil leaves

1 tsp rosemary leaves

1 tsp parsley leaves

1 tsp oregano leaves

1 tsp dill weed

1 tsp celery salt

1 - 2 T honey (I like citrus honey when I can get it, but regular will do)

1 tsp each of salt and freshly ground pepper

Combine all of these ingredients in a large bowl or a 1-gallon size zip top bag and mix well. Add meat and squeeze all of the air out if using the bag, or stir and push the meat down into the marinade until all meat is exposed to the marinade. Put in refrigerator for at least three hours or overnight, if desired. Remove meat from marinade and place directly onto a grill, without patting dry, over moderately high heat for 25 – 45 minutes. Dispose of marinade. Watch carefully to see how grill is cooking. Slow it down only if it is charring. Turn to cook all surfaces until it is as done as you like. A meat temperature of 130^0 to 145^0 is wonderful unless you must have it well done. Remove from grill and let rest for 10 minutes before slicing into 1" thick slices. (This can also be done in a 425° oven in an oiled cast iron or other ovenproof skillet. It may take a few more minutes if not browned first.)

PORK LOIN STEAKS

4 thick pork loin chops**
2 T butter
1 tsp California style garlic powder (garlic powder with parsley flakes)
1 tsp dill weed
½ tsp thyme leaves
Freshly ground sea salt
Freshly ground black pepper

Heat a large skillet over medium/high heat. Place chops in dry skillet and sear for 1-2 minutes, until meat releases from skillet. Turn chops with tongs and sear other side until meat releases from skillet. Reduce heat to medium low and add butter to skillet. Lift each chop so that butter flows under all chops. Sprinkle with dill and thyme, then season to taste with sea salt and pepper. Cook for 2-3 minutes, then turn and cook to desired doneness, approximately 3-4 minutes. Do not overcook. These are juicy and flavorful, while so quick and easy to prepare. I found Hickory sea salt in a grinder and it is awesome, but regular sea salt or salt is great, too. **This also works very well with boneless skinless chicken breasts.

GIGI'S WINNING MEATLOAF

The ingredients for the meatloaf are not exact. I use ground chuck (20% fat) for moist, tender meatloaf. Into 1 pound or so of chuck, I add 1 egg, 1–2 slices of bread, torn into small pieces, 1 small onion, diced, ½ small can of tomato sauce, and salt and pepper, to taste. Mix all of that together and form into loaf shape. The topping is a little more exact: Into the remaining ½ can of tomato sauce, add 1 tablespoon each of mustard, vinegar, and brown sugar. Mix well and pour over the meat. I bake it uncovered, at 350° for one hour. Adjust time and temperature for convection oven. I would encourage you to be more creative with the meatloaf, adding whatever your family likes (or whatever you'd like to conceal). I think it is the meat and the topping that make the difference. Submitted by Gigi Knibb.

PAN SEARED BLACKENED STEAK

2 - ¾" thick steaks or filets, 4 - 6 oz. each

2 T olive oil

2 T softened butter (mixed with 1 tsp soy sauce or Worcestershire, opt.)

½ tsp paprika

½ tsp dried basil

½ tsp rosemary

½ tsp sugar (this does not sweeten the meat but helps to caramelize for a wonderful crust)

½ tsp each freshly ground sea salt and ground black pepper

1/8 tsp cayenne, or white pepper

Combine seasonings in a small bowl. Gently pat meat dry with paper towel. Rub softened butter onto meat and sprinkle seasoning mix over all sides. Heat olive oil in a large skillet over medium high heat to almost smoking. Carefully place steaks in skillet or onto a well-heated grill plate and cook for 2 - 3 minutes or until browned. This may smoke; use your vent fan or cook outside on a grill-plate on the grill. Use a spatula to turn and cook until meat is done to your liking. This method works well for many small cuts of meat, and you can use your favorite purchased spice blend for convenience.

MARINATED LONDON BROIL

1½ - 2 lb. London Broil

1 - gallon sized plastic zip-top bag

2 T Worcestershire sauce

2 T red wine vinegar or fresh lemon juice

2 T soy sauce

¼ C cider vinegar

½ C olive oil

2 T dry parsley

½ tsp marjoram leaves

¾ tsp salt

1 tsp fresh ground pepper

5 (yes 5) large garlic cloves minced or put through a garlic press.

Combine all ingredients except the steak in the large zip-top bag. Rinse and pat dry the London broil and place in bag. Carefully squeeze out the excess air and seal. Refrigerate for at least 4 hours and as much as 24 hours, turning a couple of times to evenly marinate the meat. When ready to cook, remove from the marinade, but do not pat dry. Discard bag and marinade. Broil for 12 - 15 minutes per side, about 6 inches from the heat or grill on the barbeque approximately the same time for rare to medium. Remove from grill and let rest, under aluminum foil, for 10 to 15 minutes before slicing. Thinly slice across the grain to serve. This will serve 4 quite generously, but will also serve 2 and have enough to enjoy steak fajitas the next day. Wrap and chill leftovers.

RED CHILI BEEF

2 lb. chuck roast, cut into 1" cubes
1 C flour
½ tsp white pepper
1½ tsp salt
1 tsp oregano
1 – 2 T chili powder, to taste
½ tsp ground cumin
1 tsp dried cilantro leaves (or 3 T fresh chopped)
2 T brown sugar
1 small can tomato paste
2 small cans tomato sauce
3 – 4 cloves garlic, diced or pressed
½ green pepper, diced
1 stalk celery with leaves, diced
½ C olive oil

Shake meat cubes in flour mixed with salt and pepper. Brown in hot oil in a large heavy skillet. Stir in garlic, peppers, and celery and cook until crisp tender. Add the rest of the ingredients and stir together. Simmer for 2 hours. 30 minutes before serving, you can add 1 can of drained and rinsed kidney beans, if desired. Adjust chili powder to suit your taste. If you would like thicker gravy, stir in 1 – 2 T cornmeal at least 30 minutes before serving.

BUFFALO HASH

1 lb. ground buffalo
3 medium russet potatoes, peeled and cubed to ½"
1 – 1½ C frozen peas and carrots, or mixed vegetables, thawed
½ C diced onion, optional
½ C clarified butter (ghee)
4 - 5 cloves garlic, minced, or thinly sliced
2 tsp smoked paprika
1 T Tamari (soy) sauce
1 tsp Worcestershire sauce
Freshly ground sea salt and black pepper to taste
Cook diced potatoes in clarified butter, or ghee, over medium high heat until browned and crisp. Spoon out onto paper towels to drain, and set aside. Crumble ground buffalo in the same skillet, in the clarified butter, cooking over medium high heat until well browned, adding a little more butter or oil as needed to fry meat crisply brown. Stir in garlic and onion, if used, and cook for a minute or two until fragrant. Add thawed vegetables and soy and Worcestershire sauce, along with a tablespoon of water, and cover for 2 minutes, just to steam vegetables. Remove lid from pan and stir potatoes back into mixture just long enough to reheat, but not lose the crisp. The ghee intensifies the wonderful flavor of the buffalo and keeps it from being dry. This is Nick's favorite dish! He doesn't even request bread or dessert!

NICK'S STEAK FINGERS

2 small to medium tenderized cube steaks, partially frozen for ease in handling
1½ C buttermilk (no substitutions!)
1 C all purpose flour
½ tsp baking powder
1 tsp baking soda
½ tsp salt
½ tsp black pepper
½ tsp dried rosemary
1 tsp dried thyme
½ tsp dried basil
½ tsp garlic powder
vegetable oil for frying
Cut cube steaks into ¾" slices and gently place in a one quart zip-top

plastic bag with buttermilk. Squeeze out air, seal, and set aside to chill for 30 minutes. In a one-gallon zip top bag, combine remaining ingredients and gently add steak pieces, only letting excess buttermilk drip off, gently shaking bag when adding pieces to keep pieces floured and separated. Seal bag, gently turning once or twice while heating 2" of vegetable oil over medium high heat in a wide, heavy, deep pot until it begins to shimmer. (Approximately 365°) Carefully add meat, cooking only 4 or 5 pieces at a time, not crowding, using tongs to turn as it browns, for 3 - 5 minutes, until well browned and meat is done. Drain on paper towels and lightly salt while hot. These cook fairly rapidly and I have done homemade French fries in the vegetable oil, and then immediately fried the steak fingers in the same oil I just removed the fries from and served both, nice and hot! Do salt the fries too, immediately after frying, to keep them crisp! Serve steak fingers with cocktail or horseradish sauce, or your favorite dipping sauce, if desired.

PASTIES - MEAT FILLING

1 – 2 - 3 lb. beef rump or arm roast
¾ C beef broth
2 bay leaves
½ tsp thyme
½ tsp marjoram
1 tsp freshly ground pepper
½ tsp garlic powder
½ tsp onion salt
2 - large potatoes, peeled and cut to ½" cube
1 medium onion, diced

Brown roast in 3 T oil in hot skillet until browned on all surfaces. Transfer to a crockpot. Put broth into slightly cooled skillet and stir up any loose bits of flavor from skillet. Pour over meat in crockpot and add herbs. Cook on high for 4 hours. Cool and cut or shred meat into bite size pieces, removing any fat or undesired bits. Thicken remaining broth strained from crock pot with 4 T flour stirred into ½ C cold water, whisked in and cooked over medium heat until thickened. Taste and adjust seasoning if desired. Cool and add to meat. Set aside to chill until ready to use. When ready to make pasties, cook potatoes in a large skillet in 2 or 3 T vegetable oil until crisp and brown. Stir in diced onion and cook just until onion is crisp tender. Remove from heat. Stir in meat mixture and use this to fill pasties. Cook's notes* Leftover cubed roast beef or pork and gravy can be used. Just fry up some potatoes and onions to add to the mix and proceed with the pastry. Filling needs to be cool for ease in preparation. Pasties can be frozen and baked later for 35 to 45 minutes until golden brown and done.

CREAM CHEESE PASTRY FOR PASTIES

½ C butter, room temperature **
1- 8 oz. pkg. cream cheese, room temperature
2 C all purpose flour
5 T iced water

Cream together the butter and cream cheese with a wooden spoon. Add the flour and cut together with a table knife or pastry cutter just to pea size pieces. Add in just enough ice water to hold it together. Shape into 2 evenly sized discs and place in zip top plastic bags and chill until ready to use. When ready to use, divide each disc into 4 pieces and roll out into 6-8" circles on a lightly floured surface. Just off center place 2 – 3 T cooled meat filling onto each circle and fold pastry over filling to make a D shaped pocket.

With a fork, press edges together and poke into top 3-4 times to vent steam. Transfer to an ungreased baking sheet and bake at 400° for 15 minutes until golden brown and hot through. **Can use butter flavor shortening. Pastry can be halved.

MEXICAN DISHES

PORK AND GREEN CHILI
3 C flour
1 tsp salt
3 - 4 oz. cans diced green chilies
½ tsp white pepper
2 lb. pork tenderloin, cubed
1 small can diced tomato with green chilies
3 cloves garlic, diced
½ C olive oil

Mix flour, salt, and pepper in plastic bag and drop in pork pieces. Shake to coat. Heat oil in large skillet and brown the meat. Add garlic and stir in chilies, tomatoes, salt, and pepper. Let simmer until pork is tender, about 45 minutes, then serve hot with flour tortillas and shredded cheddar cheese for garnish. This is also a good sauce to put in or over burritos.

MEAT FILLING FOR BURRITOS
1 lb. beef, for stew, cut into ½" cubes
½ - 3/4 lb. center cut pork chops, cut into ½" cubes
1 C chopped onion
4 - 5 garlic cloves, minced
1 – 4 oz. can diced green chilies
½ tsp ground cumin
salt and pepper, to taste
1½ C water
3 T vegetable oil, for frying

In a large skillet (with a lid) heat oil over medium-high heat and cook meat chunks until brown. Add onion and garlic, salt, pepper, and water and heat until boiling, stirring up browned bits. Reduce heat to low, cover, and simmer for two hours or until meat is very tender and begins to fall apart. Add green chilies and cumin, stir, and gently flake meat. Cook, uncovered until most of the liquid has evaporated. Fill a warmed flour tortilla with meat, heated refried beans if desired, and top with grated cheese, then roll up, for a yummy burrito. This can be done in a crockpot, but it has much more flavor on top of the stove! This also makes a good filling for enchiladas.

CHICKEN AND MOZZARELLA QUESADILLAS

4 – 8" flour tortillas

½ C shredded cheddar cheese

1 C diced or shredded cooked chicken

1 tsp dried basil

1 medium tomato, diced

1 tsp olive oil

1 C shredded mozzarella

Preheat oven to 400°. Arrange tortillas in a single layer on a baking sheet and toast for 5 minutes. Turn and toast for 3 more minutes. Top 2 of the tortillas with chicken, tomatoes, mozzarella and basil. Top with another tortilla and brush lightly with oil. Sprinkle with cheddar and bake for 8-10 minutes until cheese is melted and bubbly. Cut into wedges to serve. Delicious served with beans and Spanish rice.

MEXICALI RICE

1 lb. ground beef, pork, or turkey

1 C cooked rice

1- 4 oz. can of diced green chilies

1- 10 oz. can tomatoes with chilies

¼ C chopped onions

½ tsp each salt and pepper

1 tsp chili powder

½ tsp ground cumin

1 C grated pepper jack or cheddar cheese, divided.

Fully cook meat and drain. Stir in onion and cook for additional 2 to 3 minutes. Add rice, chilies, tomatoes with chilies, spices and half of the cheese. Pour the mixture into a lightly sprayed baking dish and top with remaining cheese. Bake at 350° for 30 - 35 minutes until cheese is melted and mixture is hot. *Note. You can substitute a small jar of your favorite salsa for the tomatoes with chilies and green chilies.

BLACK BEAN SALSA

1 – 15 oz. can of black beans, rinsed and drained
1 - 10 oz. can tomatoes with chilies
1 – 15 oz. can of whole kernel corn, drained
¾ - 1 C chopped sweet onions
1 medium green pepper, chopped
2 tsp olive oil
2 tsp Balsamic vinegar
½ tsp garlic powder
1 tsp ground cumin
¾ - 1 C prepared salsa

Combine all items in a medium container. Cover and chill for at least 4 hours for the flavors to blend. Store in refrigerator in covered container. Serve with tortilla chips.

CHICKEN ENCHILADA CASSEROLE

Line a 13x9" baking pan with foil or parchment paper. Spray pan with non-stick spray and spread a thin layer of medium green enchilada sauce in the bottom. Line pan with flour tortillas, having the rounded edges come up to the top of the pan. Use as many tortillas as you need (cutting to various shapes as needed) to completely cover the bottom of the pan. Some overlapping of the tortillas is just fine. Pre-heat oven to 375^0. In a bowl, combine and lightly mix:

Meat from one store rotisserie chicken, coarsely cut up
1 container of Philadelphia Cooking Crème (Santa Fe Blend)
1 can black beans, drained and rinsed
1 can diced tomatoes with green chilies, drained
½ to 1 C of diced onions
1 small can diced green chilies (mild or medium), drained

Spoon half of above mixture onto tortillas. Cover with a thin layer of light sour cream and Mexican-blend (or all cheddar) shredded cheese. Top with more flour tortillas to cover, with the rounded edges of the tortillas again going to the top of the baking pan. Repeat with the rest of the chicken mixture, more sour cream and shredded cheese. Top with more flour tortillas to cover. Spread a moderate layer of light sour cream on top, cover with a generous coat of the medium green enchilada sauce and sprinkle more shredded cheese generously on top of all. Cover loosely with foil. Bake at least 75 minutes, then uncover and bake until the middle is heated through and cheese is golden brown. (20-30 minutes) This makes 8 very generous servings (great for a pot-luck), and also freezes very well in serving-size portions. Adapted and Submitted by Suzy LeRoy from a Philadelphia Cooking Crème Recipe.

CRISPY ENCHILADA CASSEROLE

2 C cheddar cheese, shredded
1 – 15 oz. can chili with beans
1 - 6 oz. can tomato paste
½ C water
½ C diced onion
1 - 6 oz. pkg. corn chips
1 C (8 oz.) sour cream
1 can (1 2/3 C) enchilada sauce

Combine 1½ C shredded cheddar cheese, enchilada sauce, chili, tomato paste, water, onion, and all but 1 C of the corn chips. Pour into a lightly greased baking dish. Bake, uncovered, at 375° for 30 minutes. Spread sour cream over the top of the casserole and sprinkle with ½ C shredded cheddar cheese. Make a circle around the edge of dish with remaining chips. Bake additional 5 minutes. Serve with heated refried beans and a salad with guacamole, if desired.

FAJITA FRITTATA

1 T butter or olive oil
4 eggs
½ C thinly sliced green pepper
¼ C water
½ C thinly sliced onion
2 cloves garlic, minced
1 medium tomato, sliced
1 tsp chili powder
¼ tsp ground cumin
1 C shredded cheddar
flour tortillas, salsa, and sour cream, optional
10" ovenproof skillet

Sauté pepper, onion, and garlic in butter or oil for 3-4 minutes. Stir in cumin and chili powder and remove from heat. Preheat broiler. Beat eggs until foamy. Beat in water and pour egg mixture over vegetables in pan. Cook over medium heat until eggs are almost set, approximately 6-8 minutes. Evenly place tomato slices over top of eggs and sprinkle with shredded cheddar. Broil until cheese is melted and eggs are set. Cut into wedges and serve with flour tortillas. Top with salsa and sour cream if desired.

CHILIES RELLENOS PUFF

2 – 7 oz. cans diced green chilies
8 oz. shredded Monterey jack cheese
5 eggs
2/3 C milk
6 T flour
¾ tsp baking powder
1 C shredded cheddar cheese
¼ C sunflower seeds, opt.

Beat eggs until foamy; add milk, flour and baking powder. Beat until smooth. Add chilies and cheese. Stir to mix well. Pour into a greased 9" square baking dish. Sprinkle top of mix with shredded cheddar and then sunflower seeds, if used. Bake in a preheated 375° oven for 30 minutes, or until set. Just before serving, cover top of casserole with ¼ C sliced black olives and serve with spiced tomato sauce* or fresh or prepared salsa and sour cream, as desired. *For spiced tomato sauce: 2 – 6 oz. cans tomato paste diluted with wine or water to make a thick sauce. Add ½ tsp. basil, ½ tsp. oregano, 1 crushed garlic clove, 2 tsp. brown sugar, and salt and pepper, to taste. Heat in a small saucepan until thick and hot.

MEXICAN LASAGNA

2 C small curd cottage cheese
1 C taco cheese (Fiesta or mixed cheese)
1 additional generous C taco cheese (for topping)
2 eggs
2 lbs. ground beef
1 15-oz. can refried beans
1 package taco seasoning
1 4-oz. can chopped green chilies
¼ cup prepared salsa (or more, for moisture)
1 box no bake lasagna noodles

Mix cottage cheese, 1 C taco cheese, eggs and chilies together. Set aside. Brown and drain ground beef. Add Taco seasoning and prepare according to taco seasoning directions. Add salsa and refried beans. Mix well and heat briefly, stirring occasionally. In a 9x13" pan, layer ½ beef mixture, lasagna noodles and all of the cottage cheese mixture. Cover with lasagna noodles, then remaining beef mixture, and top with plenty of taco cheese.

Bake at 350°, covered, for 30 minutes. Uncover and bake for 10 to 15 minutes more. Let stand for 5 minutes. Serve with sour cream and salsa. Serves 6 to 8. Submitted by Mabel Becker.

TACO SALAD TEXAS STYLE
1 packet taco seasoning mix**
1 lb. ground beef or turkey
1 can pinto or ranch-style beans, drained
1 bag of chopped lettuce (approximately ½ head)
1 large chopped tomato
1 (8 oz.) bag shredded Colby or cheddar cheese
1 small can of chopped black olives
½ C chopped green onions or sweet onion
½ C Catalina-style dressing
your favorite salsa
Approx. 2-3 C of Fritos or tortilla chips, lightly crushed
In skillet, brown meat and season with a packet of taco seasoning (follow pkg. directions) ** or with 1 tsp. each garlic powder, seasoning salt, chili powder and ground cumin (adjust to your taste). Drain off fat. To individual plates or a large salad bowl, layer the ingredients in the following order: lettuce, meat, beans, tomato, olives, onion and chips. Top with dressing, then cheese. Toss lightly and serve with salsa on the side. If taking to a potluck, add the chips when you get there, then toss. You can make this vegetarian by omitting the meat. It is also delicious that way (no meat) or served as a side salad along with grilled meat or chicken. I have also made it using leftover grocery store rotisserie chicken. This recipe is easily doubled or tripled for a crowd. Submitted by Chris Yust.

TACO MEAT SEASONING MIX*

1 T flour
1 T cornstarch
1 T dried minced onion
1 tsp beef bouillon or 1 cube, crushed
1 tsp garlic salt
1 tsp cumin
1 tsp dried cilantro
1 tsp paprika
1 tsp chili powder
½ tsp onion salt
¼ tsp cayenne pepper
¼ tsp sugar

*Equal to 1.25 oz. packet seasoning mix. Combine and store in airtight container.

To make taco meat: Brown 1 pound of ground beef over medium-high heat and drain. Add seasoning mix and ¾ C water. Bring to a boil. Reduce heat to medium-low. Simmer, uncovered for 10 minutes. Use to fill prepared taco shells and top with shredded cheese, lettuce, and tomatoes for an easy dinner. You can also use to fill a burrito along with beans, rice, and cheese, as desired.

LEFTOVER STEAK FOR FAJITAS

Remove leftover cooked London broil from refrigerator and slice as thinly as you can across the grain. In a large skillet sauté one each, thinly sliced onion and green pepper, in 2 T olive oil just long enough to make them crisp tender. Stir in the sliced meat along with 2 tsp chili powder, ½ tsp ground cumin, salt and pepper, to taste and ½ C of your favorite picante sauce or salsa, if desired. Bring up to a simmer and remove from heat. Spoon ½ to 1 C of the mixture onto an 8 or 9" warm flour tortilla along with ¼ C shredded cheddar cheese. Roll up or fold like a burrito and enjoy. Serve with rice and or beans if you like. (I skipped the vegetables and salsa for Nick's sake and it was still great). I just sprayed the skillet with non-stick spray, stirred in the sliced meat and added the herbs and 2 T of water. Once hot through, I added the mixture and cheese to warm tortillas. This time there were no leftovers!)

MARINATED LONDON BROIL:

1½ - 2 lb. London broil
1 - gallon size plastic zip-top bag
2 T Worcestershire sauce
2 T fresh lemon juice
2 T soy sauce
¼ C cider vinegar
½ C olive oil
2 T dry parsley
½ tsp marjoram leaves
¾ tsp salt
1 tsp fresh ground pepper
5 (yes 5) large garlic cloves, minced or put through a garlic press.

Combine all ingredients except the steak in the large zip-top bag. Rinse and pat dry the London broil and place in bag. Carefully squeeze out the excess air and seal. Refrigerate for at least 4 hours or as much as 24 hours, turning a couple of times to evenly marinate the meat. When ready to cook, remove from the marinade, but do not drain. Discard bag and marinade. Broil for 12 - 15 minutes per side about 6 inches from the heat or grill on the barbeque approximately the same time for rare to medium. Remove from grill and let rest, under aluminum foil, for 10 to 15 minutes before slicing. Thinly slice across the grain to serve. This will serve 4 quite generously, but will also serve 2 and have enough to enjoy steak fajitas the next day. Wrap and chill leftovers.

CHICKEN FAJITA MIX

1 – 1½ lbs. boneless skinless chicken or turkey breast
1 large onion, diced in chunks
2 – 3 bell peppers (use red & yellow for extra flavor), sliced thinly
½ - ¾ C key lime juice (regular lime juice is okay too, but key lime has more flavor.)
3 – 5 T chili powder, to taste

Combine key lime juice with chili powder in small glass or enamel bowl. Cut uncooked chicken or turkey breast into bite size pieces and add to chili mixture. Stir to coat all pieces, cover and chill for 15 minutes to 24 hours. Cook chicken in marinade over medium-high heat in non-stick skillet until done, about 8 minutes. Remove chicken from pan but leave marinade. Add onion to pan and cook for 10 minutes, stirring once or twice. Add peppers and cook for an additional 6 minutes, adding a little water or lime juice as needed to keep mixture juicy, 1 T at a time. Add chicken back to pan and cook for a few more minutes to completely reheat meat. This recipe makes enough fajita mix to last for several meals and freezes very well. Just seal in plastic bags in meal size portions for extra convenience. Serve with warmed tortillas, shredded Mexican cheese blend, lettuce, salsa, and sour cream for fajitas or use to make quesadillas: ½ C fajita mix and ½ C shredded cheddar placed on half of a 6 or 8" flour tortilla and heated in a very lightly oiled skillet over medium heat. Fold and heat until lightly browned and hot through. This mixture can also be added to scrambled eggs with shredded cheddar and spooned into a flour tortilla for a great breakfast burrito. Add sour cream and salsa as desired. Submitted by Diane Melde.

SALMON QUESADILLAS

2 garlic cloves, minced
1 T butter, softened
1 T olive oil
4   8 – 10" flour tortillas
1 - 6 oz. can salmon, drained*
2 C (8oz.) mozzarella, shredded
1 tsp dried basil
½ tsp freshly ground black pepper
guacamole or salsa, as desired

Sauté garlic in oil until tender. Stir in salmon, basil, and pepper. Cook over medium heat just until heated through. Meanwhile, spread butter over one side of each tortilla. Place one tortilla, butter side down, on a griddle or large skillet. Sprinkle with ½ C cheese and evenly spoon ¼ of salmon mixture over ½ of the tortilla. Fold over (in half) and cook on low for 1 – 2 minutes on each side. Two tortillas, filled and folded this way, can fit into a large skillet. Cut into wedges and serve with salsa and/or guacamole. *A small can of shrimp can be substituted for the salmon with excellent results.

FRIJOLES BORRACHOS (Drunken Beans)

1 8-oz. bag of dry pinto beans, rinsed and soaked overnight (1¼ C dried beans) OR 2 16-oz. cans of pinto beans
½ C (about 2 oz.) cubed pork shoulder (or bacon)
4 thick slices of bacon, cut into ½" pieces
2 Serrano chilies or 1 jalapeño pepper, stemmed, seeded, and sliced
salt to taste
1½ T tequila (or to taste)
¼ C chopped cilantro
If using dry pinto beans, rinse thoroughly and scoop into medium (4 qt.) pot. Add 5 cups of water, add pork shoulder (or bacon) and bring to a boil. Reduce heat and gently simmer, partially covered, until beans are very tender (about 2 hours), stirring regularly and adding water as needed to keep liquid ½" over beans. In medium skillet, fry bacon pieces until crisp. Drain on paper towels and set aside. Remove all but 2 T of drippings and stir in chopped onions and chilies. Fry until deeply golden brown and add to bean mixture. Add salt, to taste, and simmer for 20 - 30 minutes, stirring occasionally. (If too soupy, raise heat and boil, stirring frequently, to thicken.) Just before serving, stir in tequila and cilantro. Serve in warm bowls, topped with crumbled bacon. Yields 4 - 6 servings as a side dish. Submitted by Donna Clark.

TAMALE PIE

1 lb. ground beef, cooked and drained
1 onion, chopped
1 tsp garlic salt or 1 tsp minced garlic
1 15-oz. can diced tomatoes, in juice
1 8-oz. can tomato sauce
1 15-oz. can corn, undrained
1 15-oz. can medium pitted olives, undrained
1 green pepper, chopped
8 oz. cheddar cheese, shredded
¾ C yellow corn meal
1 T chili powder
¼ tsp ground pepper

Mix half of the shredded cheddar with all of the rest of the ingredients and put in a greased 2 qt. casserole. Top with remaining cheddar and bake at 350°, covered, for 30 minutes, then uncovered for an additional 30 minutes. Submitted by Pat Dunkel.

MEXICAN CHILAQUES CASSEROLE

1 – 14 oz. bag tortilla chips
½ tsp seasoned salt
1 large onion, chopped
1 – 4 oz. can diced green chilies
2 T vegetable oil
½ C shredded Parmesan cheese
1 – 18 oz. can tomatoes
8 oz. Monterey jack cheese, sliced
1 pkg. Spanish rice or taco seasoning mix
1-pint sour cream
1½ C grated cheddar cheese, divided

Sauté onion in oil until crisp tender. Add tomatoes, seasoning mix, seasoned salt, and chilies. Simmer 10 – 15 minutes. In a buttered 2 quart casserole, layer chips, sauce, Parmesan cheese, jack cheese, ½ C cheddar, and sour cream. Repeat, ending with sour cream. Bake at 350° for 30 minutes. Sprinkle with remaining cheddar and bake for additional 10 minutes.

BEER BATTER FOR FISH OR SHRIMP TACOS (OR VEGETABLES!)

1 egg

2 tsp cornstarch, plus additional for dredging

1 C flour

1 tsp baking powder

1 C beer/ale

½ tsp salt

Mix together dry ingredients. Beat egg and stir in beer, then combine with dry ingredients. Roll items of choice (white fish pieces, shrimp, vegetables, etc.) in cornstarch then dip in batter. Let excess drip off, then gently set into hot oil (365°) and cook until golden brown; drain on paper towels. For tacos, heat corn tortillas on a dry griddle and fill with shrimp or fish pieces and top with fresh lime juice, shredded cabbage and your choice of salsa, Pico de Gallo, and/or white sauce*.

SPICED YOGURT AND MAYO WHITE SAUCE FOR FISH TACOS

1 small hot chili of choice, very finely diced (habanero, jalapeno, or Serrano)

½ C plain yogurt

½ tsp ground cumin

½ C mayonnaise

½ tsp dried crushed dill

¼ tsp ground cayenne pepper

1 tsp capers, very finely diced, optional

½ tsp Mexican oregano

Fresh lime juice, as needed

Ground white pepper, to taste

Mix yogurt and mayonnaise in a bowl. Stir in fresh lime juice until slightly runny. Add chili and capers, if used. Blend in spices and adjust white pepper to taste. **You may wish to adjust the amount and type of diced chili and pepper to suit your personal taste.

CHILI-MANGO SALSA

1 large mango, peeled, pitted, and diced
¼ C fresh chopped cilantro
¼ C chopped red onion
1 T fresh lime juice
2 tsp Serrano chili, seeded, and minced
1 tsp finely grated lime zest
1 clove garlic, minced
1½ T olive oil
salt and freshly ground black pepper

In a large bowl, combine mango, cilantro, onion, lime juice, chili, lime zest, garlic and olive oil; season with salt and pepper, to taste. Chill, or let set at room temperature for at least 30 minutes to allow the flavors to blend. Serve with tortilla chips or crackers. Submitted by Cleo Collette.

SHREDDED BEEF FOR TACOS, BURRITOS, ETC.

1 3 – 5 lb. arm bone or rump roast
1 – 14.5oz. can of fire roasted diced tomatoes in juice*
2 – 4 oz. cans diced green chilies
2 bay leaves
4 garlic cloves, minced
1 large onion, diced
2 T chili powder
1 tsp ground cumin
2 T dried cilantro
2 tsp freshly ground black pepper
1 tsp Mexican oregano
½ tsp ground chipotle, optional

Just before bedtime, place roast in crockpot and top with tomatoes, chilies, onion, and garlic. Add remaining herbs and spices, cover, set on low, and let cook overnight. The next day, pick meat pieces from juices and separate and discard bay leaves, fat and gristle. Shred meat with two forks and place in a large baking or roasting pan. Pour in all of the juices and tomato bits and chilies, and roast meat at 375⁰ until browned and crispy around the edges and juices have reduced and concentrated, approximately one hour to an hour and a half, depending on how much meat juices remain. Stir occasionally while roasting and remove from oven before all the meat juices evaporate. Use immediately to fill tacos or to add into burritos, topping with your favorite fixings as desired, or cool and store in airtight containers in refrigerator for later use. Stuff your baked potatoes with this meat, topping with cheese and broiling for a few minutes and serving with salsa and sour cream, for a quick and easy meal. *Picante sauce and or RoTel sauce can be used as a short cut instead of the tomatoes and chilies when preparing meat, if desired.

SIMPLE SPANISH RICE

1 C raw long grain or Jasmine rice, rinsed until water runs clear
2 T olive oil or ghee (clarified butter)
1 C fire-roasted chopped tomatoes in juice or puree
1 tsp salt
1 T chili powder
1 C chicken broth or water

In a 1-quart heavy saucepan with a well fitting lid, heat olive oil or ghee over moderately high heat until very hot. Stir in well-drained rice and continue to stir and fry until rice begins to brown and has become milky white, about 5 to 7 minutes. Very carefully stir in water and tomatoes and add salt and chili power. Stir well and bring up to a rolling boil. Reduce heat, cover, and simmer gently for 12-14 minutes. Remove from heat but do not remove lid. Set aside to steam for 15 minutes, then gently fluff rice with a fork before serving.

MEXICAN "REFRIED" BEANS

½ lb. dry pinto beans, rinsed, picked over, and soaked overnight
1-quart water or chicken broth
1 T olive oil
½ small onion, chopped, optional
1 tsp salt
2 T chili powder
½ tsp chipotle powder, optional, for additional heat
1 clove garlic, minced
½ C salsa (or juices with tomatoes and chilies from roasting taco meat)
2 T bacon grease or 2 or 3 slices of uncooked bacon

Place beans, water or broth, olive oil, and onion if used, in a large heavy pot. Bring up to a boil, then reduce heat and simmer over low heat for 2 to 2½ or until beans are tender, adding water as needed to keep beans covered. Once beans are tender, stop adding water and stir in salt and remaining ingredients and continue cooking until liquid has reduced and beans have thickened, for at least another hour or so. Before serving, mash some (or all) of the beans with a potato masher or an immersion blender, adjust seasoning and liquid, if needed, and stir in a couple of handfuls of shredded cheddar cheese, if desired. I have made these in a crockpot, but find that the beans have a better texture and flavor when cooked on the stovetop. Once the beans have thickened and if the cheese has been added, watch your heat so as not to scorch your beans. This makes enough to serve 4 healthy appetites as a side dish and have a small amount of leftovers to add to your leftover meat and rice and make into burritos for a great follow-up dinner! (If you like Mexican food as much as I do!!) A metal simmer plate comes in handy for simmering beans and other things that need to cook at a low simmer if you find it hard to adjust the temperature of your burners. They usually have a wooden handle and can be found in the kitchen gadget department of your favorite grocery or department store. This would also be a good time to use your induction cooker for great temperature control.

MY FAVORITE FLOUR TORTILLAS

2½ C all-purpose flour

1 tsp salt (use less or no salt if using bacon grease)

1 tsp baking powder

¼ C dry non-fat milk powder

½ C lard or cold bacon fat/lard combo (or use butter or shortening)

1½ - 2 C boiling water

Whisk the flour, salt, powdered milk, and baking powder together in a mixing bowl. Mix in the lard with your fingers until the flour resembles cornmeal. Add the boiling water and mix until the dough comes together; place on a lightly floured surface and carefully (when cool enough) knead a few minutes until smooth and elastic. Place back in bowl, covered, to rest for 30 minutes. Divide the dough into 8 equal pieces and roll each piece into a ball. Preheat a large cast iron skillet over medium-high heat for several minutes. Use a well-floured rolling pin on a lightly floured surface to roll a dough ball into a thin, round tortilla. Place onto the hot dry skillet, and cook until bubbles are browning, flattening dough as bubbles rise up; then flip and continue cooking until brown on the other side. Place the cooked tortilla on a clean dishtowel, folding towel to cover the tortilla, and continue rolling and cooking the remaining dough, stacking the cooked tortillas to steam inside the towel. Serve hot and buttered with cinnamon sugar, or in your favorite recipe for burritos or fajitas. When completely cooled, store in zip top plastic bag.

MISCELLANEOUS

BLACKENING SPICE BLEND

2 tsp sweet or smoked paprika
1 tsp dried oregano
½ tsp cayenne (red) pepper
½ tsp ground cumin
½ tsp onion powder
½ tsp garlic powder
1 tsp freshly ground black pepper
1 tsp freshly ground sea salt
½ tsp brown sugar
½ tsp white sugar

Mix together in a small bowl or measuring cup and use to rub lightly oiled fish, chicken, or pork before pan searing (over medium high heat) in a small amount of olive oil and/or butter, for a very flavorful treat. Use your exhaust fan or cook on a grill, outside, because it may smoke. Depending on thickness of meat, 2-5 minutes per side should do the job.

SIMPLE DRY SPICE RUB

1 T dried, crushed parsley
1 T garlic powder
1 T dried, crushed thyme
1 T onion powder
1 T dried, crushed oregano
1 T brown or white sugar
1 T paprika, sweet, or smoked
½ tsp freshly ground black pepper
1 T dried, crushed rosemary, optional*
1 tsp dried dill, optional*
1 tsp freshly ground sea salt
(Add heat with 1/8th - ½ tsp cayenne)

Mix all together and store in airtight container. To use, spoon out 1 or 2 T and rub over meat. Seal meat in a zip-top plastic bag, squeezing out the air, and chill, overnight. Grill or bake meat until done. *These 2 herbs are better on pork, chicken, or fish, rather than beef. Replace with 1 tsp marjoram for beef. The remaining ingredients are really great on ribs, before baking or grilling.

PASTA DISHES

ANCHOVY GARLIC AIOLI

8 oz. uncooked angel hair pasta
Water for boiling pasta
1 – 2 oz. can flat anchovies, in olive oil
8 – 10 cloves garlic, minced or pressed
3 – 5 T good quality olive oil
1 tsp. crushed red chili peppers
1 tsp. dried basil leaves
¼ to ½ tsp. chipotle chili powder
¾ tsp. freshly ground sea salt
1 tsp. freshly ground black pepper
4 – 6 oz. Parmesan cheese, freshly grated

Simple, simple, simple. Let's assemble our ingredients and get the water for the pasta going. Oh, and set the table. This really is incredibly fast, once you get started. Once your water is boiling, salt it and add in your pasta. I like to break my angel hair in half, carefully, and set it in my colander while waiting for the water to boil. Then, when the water is boiling, I pick it up and gently drop portions of it into the boiling water, crisscrossing it as it falls to help keep it from sticking together in clumps. Give it a stir, then set up your ingredients and open your anchovies. Carefully. These little cans are sharp. Next, peel and mince your garlic. Start your largest skillet heating, over medium high heat, and add in a couple of tablespoons of good olive oil. When the oil gets hot, add in the garlic and the crushed red chilies. As it becomes fragrant, add in the basil and chipotle powder. Stir and enjoy the aroma for a moment or two. Now it's time to add in the anchovies, in their oil. Mash them up with the back of a wooden spoon and stir the garlic, oil, and herbs all together. Check your pasta. It should be really close; you only want it al dente. Drain thoroughly and stir it into the skillet, adding a bit more olive oil, as needed, to keep it from sticking badly while you stir and sauté everything together. Grind some sea salt and black pepper over all and stir in a couple of handfuls of freshly grated Parmesan. Serve immediately. If you have fresh basil leaves, grab a couple and slice very thinly and toss with or over the pasta just before serving for an extra special touch! I usually grate about 3 cups of Parmesan to have plenty available to pass at the table, too! Serves 2 to 4. Pairs well with a Caesar salad.

ZESTY TOMATO SAUCE (FOR PIZZA & PASTA)

1 - 14.5 oz. can of petite cut (fire roasted) tomatoes
1 - 6 oz. can tomato paste
3 T extra virgin olive oil
3 tsp dried leaf basil, crushed
1 scant tsp freshly ground sea salt
1 - 2 tsp freshly ground black pepper; use more for heat, as desired
½ tsp dried leaf oregano
2 T dried parsley
½ tsp garlic powder (not garlic salt)

Stir all ingredients together in a glass bowl. Cover with plastic and let rest at room temperature for one hour for flavors to blend. This simple sauce can be used for a pizza topping, pasta or dipping sauce. It does not need to be cooked but can be heated to use for a pasta sauce. This sauce freezes well. I like to divide it into thirds when used for pizza topping, one to use now and two to store in the freezer in glass jars or zip top bags for later use. Thaw in refrigerator overnight.

HERB TOMATO SAUCE FOR SPAGHETTI

6 – 8 cloves garlic, minced or pressed
3 or 4 T extra virgin olive oil
2 – 6oz. cans tomato paste
1 – 28oz. can crushed tomatoes in purée
1 – 15 oz. can tomato sauce
1 – 14.5 oz. can chicken broth (or 1 C water & ¼ to ½ C red wine)
2 bay leaves
1 tsp sugar, optional
1 tsp each freshly cracked pepper and sea salt, or to taste
1 tsp chili powder
2 T crushed dried basil leaves
½ tsp dried oregano leaves
2 T dried parsley leaves
¼ tsp white pepper or 2 shakes of Tabasco

For herb tomato sauce, sauté garlic in olive oil just until slightly golden and aromatic. Spoon in tomato paste by tablespoon into hot oil and sauté for 2 - 3 minutes longer, stirring so it doesn't burn. Add crushed tomatoes in puree, sauce, and chicken broth. To this mixture, add bay leaves, sugar, salt, pepper, chili powder, basil leaves, oregano leaves, parsley, and white pepper or Tabasco. Simmer, uncovered, for at least 30 minutes for the flavors to blend or up to several hours longer for a thicker, more flavorful sauce. Can add more water or wine if it gets too thick. If adding cooked sausage or cooked meatballs to sauce, do not add liquids after adding meat, and simmer for at least 30 to 60 minutes more to combine flavors.

LINGUINE WITH HAM & CHEESE SAUCE

1 – 8 oz. pkg. linguine
2 T butter
1 small onion, chopped
1 T flour
½ tsp salt
¼ tsp freshly ground black pepper
2 C milk
1 – 4 oz. pkg. sliced cooked ham, cut into thin strips.
1 – 10 oz. pkg. frozen peas
½ C (2 oz.) shredded Swiss cheese

Prepare linguine as directed on package. Drain and return to pot, cover and keep warm. In a large heavy saucepan over medium heat, sauté onion in butter. Stir in flour, salt, and pepper until blended. Cook for 1 minute and gradually add milk, stirring constantly until thickened and smooth. Stir in frozen peas, separating with your spatula or spoon. Heat to boiling, reduce heat, and cook mixture for 2 to 3 minutes until peas are tender. Add ham and heat through. Remove saucepan from heat and stir in cheese until melted. Add linguine to pot and gently sir together. Serve immediately. Serves 4.

ITALIAN-STYLE TUNA CASSEROLE

3 T butter
2 cloves garlic, minced
1 medium onion, chopped
1 – 15 oz. can chopped tomatoes in tomato sauce
1 – 8 oz. can tomato puree
1 tsp salt
½ tsp oregano
½ tsp basil
1 – 9.25 oz. can tuna, drained (2 – 5 oz. cans)
3 C cooked egg noodles
1 C shredded cheddar or mozzarella cheese

Cook onions and garlic in butter until tender. Add tomatoes, tomato puree, salt, oregano, and basil and simmer, uncovered, for 20 minutes. Break tuna into chunks and add to sauce. Add noodles and ¾ C cheese and turn into a lightly greased casserole. Sprinkle with remaining cheese and bake at 375⁰ for 25 minutes. Serves 6.

MY FAVORITE GOULASH

3 T butter
1 clove garlic, minced
1 onion, chopped
½ green pepper, chopped
½ C celery, chopped
1 lb. lean ground beef, cooked and drained
3 – 4 C cooked macaroni
1 small can tomato sauce
1 can diced tomatoes in sauce
½ tsp each salt and pepper
1 C shredded cheddar cheese

Sauté vegetables in butter until tender and beginning to brown. Add in tomatoes and salt and pepper and simmer for 10 to 15 minutes. Add cooked ground beef to tomato mixture and simmer for 5 minutes more. Gently stir in macaroni and cheese and pour into a buttered casserole. Optionally top with additional shredded cheese and crushed potato chips or cracker crumbs, if desired. Bake at 350⁰ for 40 minutes.

PEPPERONI MACARONI

2½ C uncooked elbow macaroni
1 lb. bulk Italian sausage
1 large onion, diced
1 - 15 oz. can pizza sauce
1 - 8 oz. can tomato sauce
1/3 C milk
1 - 3½ oz. pkg. sliced pepperoni, halved
1 - 4 oz. jar sliced mushrooms, drained
1 - 2¼ oz. can sliced ripe olives, drained
1 C shredded mozzarella cheese

Cook macaroni according to directions. Meanwhile, in a skillet, over medium heat, cook sausage and onion until meat is no longer pink; drain. Drain macaroni. In a large bowl, combine pizza sauce, tomato sauce, and milk. Stir in sausage mixture, macaroni, pepperoni, mushrooms, and olives. Transfer to a greased 13X9" baking dish. Cover and bake at 350° for 30 minutes. Uncover and sprinkle with cheese. Bake for 10-15 minutes longer until bubbly and cheese is melted. Serves 8-10. Submitted by Pat Lewis.

SKILLET FRANKS WITH MACARONI

2 C water
1 - 8 oz. can tomato sauce
1 tsp. Italian herb seasoning
½ tsp. Worcestershire sauce
½ tsp. sugar
½ tsp. cayenne pepper
1 C dry macaroni
4 franks

Place first six ingredients into medium skillet and bring to a boil. Stir in macaroni. Reduce heat to a simmer and cover. Cook, covered, for about 20 minutes or until macaroni is tender. Cut franks into bite size pieces. Add to skillet and heat for another 5 minutes or so until hot. Serves 4. Submitted by Bonnie Bellomo.

VI'S MACARONI AND CHEESE

1½ C uncooked elbow macaroni
1½ T dried parsley flakes
¼ C butter
1½ T diced pimiento
1½ C shredded cheddar/jack cheese
1½ T minced onion
2 eggs
1 tsp. salt
2 C milk
½ tsp. pepper
½ tsp. paprika

Cook macaroni as directed on package. Drain, rinse in cold water, and drain again. Place in oiled casserole dish and add butter, cheese, onion, parsley, pimiento, and seasonings. Gently stir until mixed together. Beat eggs slightly and stir in milk. Pour over macaroni mixture and bake at 325° for 50 minutes until heated through and golden brown on top. Can sprinkle with crushed potato chips or crushed butter crackers 15 minutes before end of baking time.

10-MINUTE LASAGNA

1 – 26 oz. jar of pasta sauce
1 – 30 oz. bag of frozen ravioli, unthawed
8 oz. shredded mozzarella cheese
½ C grated Parmesan cheese
1 – 10 oz. pkg. frozen spinach, thawed and drained

Heat oven to 350°. Spray a 9X13" pan with nonstick spray. Spoon 1/3 of the sauce over the bottom of baking pan. Arrange ½ of ravioli over sauce, and then scatter spinach evenly over ravioli. Top with ½ of each of the cheeses, then remaining ravioli, sauce and cheese. Bake for 30 – 35 minutes until bubbly. Serve with salad and garlic toast if desired. Submitted by Nancy Benjamin.

A HANDY TIP

I love lasagna but hated cooking the noodles. Layer your lasagna in the non-stick sprayed crockpot using uncooked noodles - just break them apart to fit. I make 3 layers. Then start on high for about an hour and reduce to low for 3 hours/or until noodles are tender. So good, and easy! Submitted by Jean Watson.

SPICY SAUSAGE TORTELLINI

1 19 oz. pkg. hot Italian sausage
1 - 6 oz. can tomato paste
1 - 14.5 oz. can petite-diced tomatoes
1 - 8 oz. can tomato sauce
4 cloves garlic, minced
1 T dried parsley flakes
1 T dried basil flakes
1 tsp freshly ground black pepper
1 bay leaf
1 pkg. (serves 3 - 4) 4 cheese tortellini

Remove casing from sausage and in a large skillet or saucepan, break apart sausage, cooking over medium high heat, stirring until browned and cooked through. Drain any excess grease, reduce heat to medium low and add tomato products, garlic, and spices. Simmer for at least 20 minutes; longer is better. Cook tortellini according to package directions. Drain and serve with spicy sauce and freshly grated Parmesan. Add a salad and garlic toast and enjoy. This is also great if you combine tortellini, sauce, ½ C shredded Parmesan, and 1½ C shredded mozzarella in a sprayed casserole and bake at 350° for 30 minutes, until bubbly.

PIES

SINGLE PIE CRUST
1 1/3 C flour
¼ tsp baking powder
1 T brown sugar
1 tsp salt
1 egg, lightly beaten
2 tsp white vinegar
1/3 C lard or butter, chilled
ice water, as needed (5-8 T total)

Combine flour, baking powder, brown sugar, and salt in a mixing bowl. Use a whisk to combine and fluff dry ingredients. Cut in the lard with pastry cutter, just until crumbly, with pea sized pieces of fat left in the mixture. Mix beaten egg and vinegar together with 3 T ice water and stir into flour mixture with a fork. Add more ice water, if needed, a tablespoon at a time, JUST UNTIL MOISTENED. (Some dry mix left is okay.) Dump onto a large square of plastic wrap and use the plastic to push all of the pieces together to form a ball. Flatten ball into a smooth disc, rolling the edge on the counter to smooth it out, fold the plastic over to seal, and put in refrigerator for at least 30 minutes. To Double Crust Recipe: Use same procedure, but once dough has come together, divide into two discs, wrap and chill. When chilled, roll out with a floured rolling pin on a lightly floured surface, to between 1/8 and 3/16" thick. Roll up onto rolling pin, or fold and gently place into pie plate, folding over and crimping edge decoratively for a single crust or filling and topping with second crust, and then folding and crimping edges before baking. To blind bake (prebake) your pie crust, place a 12" square of aluminum foil onto the surface of the crust and put a layer of dry beans, rice, or pastry beads over the foil. Bake at 375° degrees (convection is okay) for 15 minutes. Remove foil and weights and bake for another 5 – 10 minutes or until golden brown. Cool completely.

GRAHAM CRACKER CRUST
1¼ C graham cracker crumbs
3 T sugar
5 T butter, melted
Combine cracker crumbs and sugar in a mixing bowl. With a fork, stir in melted butter, until well mixed. Press into the bottom and up the sides of a pie plate, using the bottom of a small measure or the bowl of a large spoon to press down firmly. Bake at 350⁰ for 10 - 12 minutes, until just barely browned and cool completely before using.

QUICK COCONUT CREAM PIE
1 – 1.5 oz. package fat-free, sugar-free instant vanilla pudding mix
1½ C cold milk (1%)
1 – 8 oz. carton thawed whipped topping
¾ - 1 C flaked coconut, toasted
1 prepared pie shell, regular or graham cracker
Beat pudding mix and cold milk together for 2 minutes. Fold in half of the whipped topping and half of the toasted coconut. Pour into crust and top with remaining whipped topping. Sprinkle with remaining toasted coconut and chill. Submitted by Joyce Mlekush.

BLACK RASPBERRY SOUR CREAM PIE
1 9" unbaked pie shell
1 T melted butter
¼ C breadcrumbs
5 T flour
1 C sugar
4 C black raspberries
2 T sugar
¼ tsp salt
1 C (8 oz.) sour cream
Combine 1 C sugar, sour cream, flour and salt. Place berries in unbaked pie shell and spread sour cream mixture over berries. Mix breadcrumbs and 2 T sugar together. Add melted butter and stir. Sprinkle crumbs over top of sour cream and berries. Bake at 375° for 40-45 minutes. Submitted by Don Hankins.

SOUR CREAM LEMON PIE

1 C sugar
1 C milk
3 T cornstarch
3 egg yolks
¼ C butter or margarine
1 C sour cream
1 T grated lemon zest
1 C whipped topping
¼ C lemon juice
1 – 9" piecrust, baked

Combine sugar and cornstarch in medium sized saucepan. Add butter or margarine, lemon zest and juice, milk, and egg yolks. Cook and stir over medium heat until the mixture comes to a boil and thickens. Remove from heat and fold in the sour cream. Cool slightly and pour into baked and cooled piecrust. Top with whipped topping and refrigerate.

CHOCOLATE CHIP PECAN PIE

3 eggs
¾ C packed brown sugar
¾ C honey
¼ C butter, melted
½ C or so chocolate chips (Hershey's Special Dark works nicely)
About 2 C pecans halves & pieces
9" unbaked deep pie crust

Preheat oven to 350⁰. In a medium bowl, mix eggs and sugar. Add honey, melted butter, and pecans. Mix until all ingredients are thoroughly combined. Spread chocolate chips across bottom of pie shell. Pour egg mixture over chocolate chip layer. Bake in preheated oven for 35 – 50 minutes. You may need to cover edges of crust (with foil) towards end of baking to keep from overcooking. Serve warm or cool with a dollop of whipped cream and a sprinkling of chocolate chips if desired. You can substitute corn syrup for part of the honey and/or white sugar for the brown. (Original recipe called for corn syrup, no honey, and white, not brown, sugar. The honey and brown sugar are my modifications along with lots of pecans.) Marie Callender makes a nice frozen pie shell that works quite well for this if you don't want to make your own. *This pie bakes just fine in the microwave/convection oven found in many motorhomes. Submitted by Diane Melde.

CUSTARD PIE

1 C sugar (can use Splenda Measure)
1 T lemon juice
3 eggs
¼ C butter, soft
3 T flour pinch of salt
1 (13 oz.) can evaporated milk (fat frcc is okay)

Beat all ingredients except evaporated milk until well blended. Slowly add the can of evaporated milk while beating continuously. Pour into a greased pie plate and bake at 350° for 45 - 60 minutes or until brown and puffy. Cool slightly before serving. Makes 4 generous servings or 6 regular ones. Best to keep in the refrigerator. Can be reheated in the microwave before serving. Submitted by Lee and Linda Branum.

CHOCOLATE CREAM PIE

Crust: (Purchased graham cracker crust, <u>OR)</u>
1¼ C finely crushed graham cracker crumbs
¼ C sugar
5 T melted butter
Filling:
1/3 C hot water
2 T unsweetened cocoa powder
1 T vanilla
8 oz. bittersweet chocolate chunks (1 1/3 C)
1½ C heavy cream
1 T sugar
1/8 tsp salt
Topping:
1 C heavy cream
3 T powdered sugar
½ tsp vanilla

Crust: Combine crumbs and sugar, and with a fork, stir in melted butter until well blended. Press firmly onto bottom and up sides of a 9" pie pan and bake at 350° for 10-12 minutes until barely browned. Cool completely.

Filling: Combine hot water, cocoa, and 1 T vanilla in a small bowl and set aside. Microwave the chocolate chunks on high for 1 minute. Stir until completely melted and let cool. Whip the cream, sugar, and salt with an electric mixer until soft peaks form. Stir the cocoa mixture into the melted chocolate, and using a whisk, fold the cooled chocolate mixture into the whipped cream until blended. Gently spoon filling into crust and smooth top. Chill for at least an hour for filling to firm up.

Topping: Whip the heavy cream, vanilla, and powdered sugar together to soft peaks. Dollop or spread the whipped cream on top of pie to serve. Chill leftovers, if you have any!

SIMPLE EGGNOG PIE

1 - prepared 9" graham cracker piecrust
2 - (3.4 oz.) packages vanilla instant pudding mix
1¼ C eggnog
6 T dark rum (optional) great without it
¼ tsp ground nutmeg
1 - 8 oz. tub whipped topping
Dash each of cinnamon, nutmeg, and sugar

Combine pudding mix, eggnog, rum (if used), and nutmeg, blending with mixer for one minute. Fold in whipped topping and spoon into crust. Sprinkle with cinnamon, nutmeg, and sugar to taste, and refrigerate for two hours or overnight. Submitted by Jo Padget.

CREAMY SUMMER LIME PIE

1 - 9" prepared graham cracker crust

1 - 8 oz. package cream cheese, at room temp

1 - 10-oz jar lime curd (1¼ cup)

2 tsp finely grated lime zest, plus more for garnish if desired

2 T lime juice

2 C heavy cream

¼ C powdered sugar

1 tsp vanilla

½ C fresh raspberries (optional, for garnish and/or serving)

In a large bowl, beat cream cheese, lime curd, grated lime zest, and lime juice with an electric mixer until light and fluffy. In another large bowl, beat whipping cream until soft peaks form. Add powdered sugar and vanilla. Beat until stiff peaks form. Fold about ¼ of the whipped cream into cream cheese mixture to soften, then fold in remaining whipped cream. Spoon into crust and chill pie for at least an hour until firm. To serve, sprinkle with fresh raspberries and additional lime zest, if you like. Chill leftovers.

LO-CAL REFRIGERATOR PIE

1 - 9" prepared graham cracker crust (see first recipe, but reduce sugar amount)

1 - 6-8 oz. container sugar free yogurt, flavor of your choice

1 - 3 oz. package sugar free gelatin, matching flavor

¼ C boiling water

½ C ice cubes

1 - 8 oz. tub of frozen whipped topping, defrosted

In 2 C measuring cup, pour boiling water gently over gelatin, stirring until gelatin is completely dissolved. Add ice cubes and stir until completely melted, then whisk in yogurt until blended. Pour mixture into a larger bowl and gently fold in whipped topping, stirring just until combined. Spoon into prepared crust and chill for at least one hour, or until firm. This low calorie pie has a wonderful chiffon texture, and well-drained fruit, (such as a small can of mandarin oranges with orange yogurt and orange gelatin, cherries with cherry yogurt and gelatin, etc.), can be stirred into filling before spooning into prepared crust for a special treat. Chill leftovers.

FRESH STRAWBERRY PIE

For crust:
1/3 C all purpose flour
¼ tsp baking powder
¼ tsp salt
1 T brown sugar
1 egg, lightly beaten
2 tsp white vinegar
1/3 C lard, chilled (butter is okay)
ice water, as needed (5-8 T total)
For Filling:
2 qt. fresh strawberries, cleaned
1 C sugar
¾ C water
3 T cornstarch or 3 T instant cleargel
1 T lemon juice

For the crust, whisk together the flour, salt, baking powder and brown sugar. Cut in the lard with pastry cutter, just until crumbly, with pea sized pieces of fat left in the mixture. Mix beaten egg and vinegar together with 3 T ice water and stir into flour mixture with a fork. Add more ice water, if needed, a tablespoon at a time, JUST UNTIL MOISTENED. (Some dry mix left is okay.) Dump onto a large square of plastic wrap and use the plastic to push all of the pieces together to form a ball. Flatten ball into a smooth disc, fold the plastic over to seal, and put in refrigerator for at least 30 minutes. When chilled, roll out with a floured rolling pin on a lightly floured surface, to between 1/8 and 3/16" thick. Roll up onto rolling pin, or fold and gently place into pie plate, folding over and crimping edge decoratively. Place a 12" square of aluminum foil onto the surface of the crust and put a layer of dry beans, rice, or pastry beads over the foil. Bake at 375° degrees (convection is okay) for 15 minutes. Remove foil and weights and bake for another 5 - 10 minutes or until golden brown. Cool completely.

For the filling, mash 1/3 of the strawberries and put into a saucepan with the water. In a small bowl, whisk together the sugar and cornstarch or cleargel. (I prefer using 2T of each.) Add to mashed berries and cook over medium heat, stirring gently, until mixture thickens. Stir in lemon juice. Cool. Place remaining berries, whole or sliced, in cooled pie shell, and evenly pour cooled filling over. Chill for at least 2 hours. Slice and serve, topped with whipped cream.

FRESH STRAWBERRY PUDDING PIE

1 prepared pie shell
2 C sliced strawberries
1 - 4-serving package cook and serve, sugar-free, fat-free, vanilla pudding mix
1 – 4-serving package sugar-free, strawberry flavored gelatin
2 C water

Combine pudding mix and gelatin with water in a saucepan and cook, stirring constantly, until mixture comes to a boil. Remove from heat and cool. Gently combine with strawberries and pour into prepared pie shell. Chill. Serve with whipped topping or whipped cream. Submitted by Joyce Mlekush

SKILLET FRUIT PIE

6 apples, pears, or peaches, peeled, cored, and sliced as for pie
3 T butter
3 T cornstarch
¼ tsp salt
1 tsp cinnamon
¼ tsp nutmeg (optional)
3 T white or brown sugar
Crust:
1 C flour
2 T shortening
2 T white sugar
6 T butter
3 – 4 T ice-cold water
Dash salt

Combine flour, dash salt, and 2 T white sugar in medium bowl. Cut in butter and shortening just to pea size. Stir in enough cold water to form a ball. Cover and chill while you prepare filling. In a large oven safe skillet, melt 3 T butter. Stir in fruit and white or brown sugar and cook for 1 minute. Add cornstarch, cinnamon, and nutmeg, if used, and stir, cooking just to crisp tender. On lightly floured surface, roll out pastry to fit your skillet size. Transfer onto hot fruit and quickly cut across pastry in a crosshatch (#) to expose more edges to crisp. Sprinkle lightly with more white sugar and put into preheated 400⁰ oven for 20 minutes to brown crust. Serve warm with vanilla ice cream.

QUICK AND EASY TURNOVER

Cleo Collette, a good friend and subscriber from Oregon, states....
I picked about 2 cups berries while waiting for something to start, plus I had some blueberries in the freezer and a nectarine that needed using, so I got a ready-made pie crust (they can make them better than I can), mixed up the fruit with a tablespoon of cornstarch and about 1/3 to 1/2 cup sugar and piled it in the middle of one half of the pie crust. I folded the crust over, pinched the edges together, cut a couple of slits in the top and brushed it with milk, sprinkled a bit of sugar on it, and baked it at 350^0 for 25 or 30 minutes, until the crust was nice and brown. It made a nice, big turnover and used up odds and ends of fruit. Try it if you get a chance.

LAZY PERSON'S COBBLER

½ C (1 cube) butter
1 C flour
1 C sugar
2 tsp baking powder
¾ C milk
1 large can (1 lb.) OR 2 C fresh fruit, prepared and cut into bite size pieces
pinch salt
Melt butter in large baking dish. Use any canned and drained OR fresh fruit. Cherries, peaches, blackberries, and blueberries take honors. Bing cherries make raves! Put fruit in pan on top of melted butter. Mix together flour, sugar, salt, and baking powder and add in milk. Stir until combined and pour or spoon mixture over fruit. Bake for 40 minutes at 375^0. Serve hot with ice cream.

MOCK APPLE PIE (Made With Zucchini!)

1 single 9" unbaked pie crust
4 C sliced zucchini
1½ tsp cream of tartar
1¼ C sugar
¾ tsp nutmeg
2 T all purpose flour
2 T lemon juice
1½ tsp ground cinnamon
¼ tsp salt
¾ C golden (or regular) raisins (optional)
¾ C chopped pecans or walnuts (optional)

Peel zucchini and cut in half, lengthwise. Remove seeds with the back of a spoon, leaving a slight scooped out area. Cut halves into slices, like apples. Sauté' in a lightly sprayed skillet or cook in the microwave until barely tender, drain, then place in cold water for 5 minutes. Drain well and add to combined remaining ingredients, along with raisins and/or nuts, if used. Gently stir together, then pour into a 9" unbaked pie crust.

Top with Crumb Topping:
½ tsp ground cinnamon
¼ tsp salt
1 C all purpose flour
1 tsp vanilla
½ C brown sugar, packed
½ C melted butter
1 tsp baking powder
1 egg, beaten with vanilla

Stir together flour, sugar, baking powder, salt, and cinnamon with fork. Stir in egg mixture until crumbly. Sprinkle evenly over pie. Pour melted butter over all. Bake at 375⁰ for 40-50 minutes until crust edges are deeply golden brown. This pie is wonderful! My dear friend Mildred Householder gave me this recipe in 1993 and I've had people tell me it's the best apple pie they have ever tasted! I don't argue.

NO ROLLING PIN PECAN PIE

½ C (1 stick) butter
½ C brown sugar, packed
1 C all purpose flour plus more, for mixing
1 C light corn syrup
3 large eggs
1 tsp vanilla
½ C white sugar
1½ C pecan halves

Melt butter in a 9" pie plate. Preheat oven to 350°. Stir 1 C flour into butter with a fork, then add more flour, as needed, just until no oily pools remain. Using floured fingers, press dough around bottom and sides of pie plate, forming a decorative edge. In a separate bowl, whisk together the eggs, sugars, corn syrup, and vanilla. Evenly spread pecans over piecrust, then pour in egg mixture. Bake for 30 minutes or until pie has set up and pie crust is toasty brown.

PIZZA

EASY PIZZAS FOR TWO

4 – 8" flour tortillas
6 T prepared pizza sauce
1 C cheddar blend cheese (Taco Mix)
1½ C shredded mozzarella cheese
Misc. options for toppings. Use any, or all, of your favorite items:
½ - 3 oz. package pepperoni slices
½ C cooked sliced or crumbled sausage
2 T diced onions, lightly cooked
2 T diced green peppers, lightly cooked
2 T sliced canned or fresh mushrooms, cooked
2 T sliced black olives

Spray heavy 10 – 12" skillet with non-stick spray then wipe with paper towel. Place one tortilla in skillet and top with ½ of cheddar blend cheese. Top with another tortilla. Spread with 3 T pizza sauce. Top with any number of optional toppings, ending with mozzarella cheese. Place lid on skillet and place over med/low heat until cheese on top is melting and bottom is crisply browned to your liking. This is easily doubled or tripled and also works quite well on the grill. Submitted by Janet & Brad Barnes.

SPEEDY PIZZA

Zesty Tomato Sauce (1/3 recipe)
½ white onion, cut into slices, then halved
¼ green pepper cut into thin slices
3 – 4 mushrooms, sliced thinly
Pepperoni slices, as desired
1 - 2 C shredded mozzarella
2 tsp olive oil
1 T sliced back olives
Split muffins, pita pocket bread, flour tortillas, halved French or garlic bread loaf, or purchased pizza bread.

In small skillet or saucepan, heat olive oil and stir in onions, peppers, and mushrooms. Stir-fry just until crisp tender and mushrooms have released their juices. Set aside to cool. Lightly brush your choice of bread with olive oil, place on baking sheet, and toast in 400° oven or toaster oven for 2-3 minutes, just until golden. Remove from oven and top with sauce, then vegetable mix and olives. Sprinkle with shredded mozzarella, top with pepperoni, then return to oven and heat until cheese is melted or browned to your liking.

ZESTY TOMATO SAUCE

1 - 14.5 oz. can of petite cut tomatoes
1 - 6 oz. can tomato paste
3 T extra virgin olive oil
3 tsp dried leaf basil, crushed
1 scant tsp freshly ground sea salt
2 tsp freshly ground black pepper
½ tsp dried leaf oregano
2 T dried parsley
½ tsp garlic powder (not garlic salt)

Stir all ingredients together in a glass bowl. Cover with plastic and let rest at room temperature for one hour for flavors to blend. It does not need to be cooked but can be heated for a pasta sauce. This sauce freezes well. I like to divide into thirds for pizza topping, one to use now and two to store in the freezer in glass jars or zip top bags for later use. Thaw in refrigerator overnight.

NICK'S FAVORITE PIZZA – PLEASE READ THROUGH – THIS RECIPE SOUNDS COMPLICATED, BUT IT IS FAIRLY SIMPLE AND SO WORTH THE TIME AND EFFORT YOU PUT INTO IT!!! DO PLAN AHEAD; THERE ARE A FEW EASY STEPS INVOLVED IN THE PREPARATION AND A FEW DAYS OF WAITING FOR THE DOUGH TO CHILL AND BUILD ITS FLAVOR, FOR THE VERY BEST RESULTS!!!

NICK'S FAVORITE PIZZA DOUGH

¼ C warm (110°) water
½ tsp instant (bread machine) yeast
½ tsp sugar, honey, or agave
1 tsp sea salt
1 tsp olive oil
2 – 3 C Sir Lancelot, Bounce, or other high gluten, high protein flour (regular flour is just okay) Combine warm water and sweetener of your choice with yeast (regular yeast will work) and let get foamy for 5 – 10 minutes. Stir together salt and 1 C flour in a large bowl. Set aside. When yeast mixture is nice and foamy, add 1 tsp olive oil and ¾ C <u>cold</u> water and stir into flour and salt. Stir into a nice dough, adding flour only as necessary to make a soft and supple, slightly tacky but not sticky, dough. Your current humidity will determine the amount of flour you will need. In bowl or on a lightly greased surface, knead for 8 – 10 minutes, then place in a well-oiled bowl with a lid, at least twice as big as your dough ball. Refrigerate for at least 5 hours, but it just gets better with time, so please wait at least 3 days and up to10 days (I've done 2 weeks with no issues). For 2 medium thickness crusts, divide in half and use two bowls (Or 3 bowls for thin and crispy crusts.) Once the dough is refrigerated, it begins to remember its shape and it is easier to press out into a circle if it starts out as a nice ball (or two or three). This will make 2 - 12" medium thickness or 1 large medium pizza crust. (3 – thin crust.) When ready for pizza, gently dump dough ball directly onto a well oiled or oil and semolina or cornmeal sprinkled pizza pan, parchment paper circle (my preference), or pizza peel. Let come to room temp, then <u>without kneading</u>, gently press out from the center, leaving a thicker edge, to your preferred thickness. Let rest for 20 – 30 minutes to rise a bit if you like a tender, chewy crust. Top with your favorite sauce and other toppings (<u>see hints below</u>) and bake in pre-heated HOT (375-500° depending on your oven's heating ability) oven until done and crispy brown (8-15 minutes), depending on temperature and toppings, preferably directly on a hot pizza

stone that has been pre-heated as the oven pre-heats for a minimum of 30-45 minutes!

QUICK AND EASY NO COOK PIZZA SAUCE FOR NICK'S PIZZA

1 (14 oz.) can Muir Glen fire roasted chopped tomatoes
1 T extra-virgin olive oil
1 tsp red wine vinegar
2 medium garlic cloves, minced
1 tsp salt and 1/4 tsp ground black pepper
1 tsp each dried oregano and basil
1 T tomato paste

Stir together all ingredients or for a smooth sauce, place in a food processor and blend for about 30 seconds. I put the garlic and a portion of the tomatoes, with some of their juice, into a mini processor, dump into a bowl and then process remaining tomatoes and stir all together. If you like a chunky sauce, leave remaining tomatoes unprocessed and just stir in the herbs, etc. Prepare a couple of hours before needed and refrigerate until ready to use. Makes enough for 3 pizzas.

**Hints for preparing Nick's pizza:

1. Use quality sliced provolone cheese as your base layer on your prepared pizza dough, and then top with sauce, then veggies, meats, freshly grated good quality parmesan cheese, finishing off with a layer of sliced good quality mozzarella.

2. Pre-bake your pepperoni on a rimmed baking sheet for 10 minutes in the oven as it is preheating and use paper towels to soak up all that extra grease, and place on pizza over sauce. (And under cheese.) Follow sausage directions to pre-cook and drain before using.

3. Pre-cook your vegetables (microwave for 3-4 minutes or quickly stir fry in lightly oiled skillet and let cool) to keep from having a soggy pizza with half-done veggies. I like to slice 2-3 big mushrooms and sauté until juices release, then add 1 large shallot, sliced thinly, and ¼ diced zucchini or ¼ julienned green pepper and stir fry just to crisp tender to top 1 - 12" pizza. If you like lots of veggies on your thick crust pizza, you may wish to par-bake your dough for 6 to 8 minutes before topping so everything gets cooked through!

4. For ease in getting your topped pizza into the oven and onto the hot stone

without a mess, prepare it on high quality parchment paper circle that has been lightly oiled (and sprinkled with semolina if desired) and slide paper and pizza together onto hot stone with a pizza peel or from the bottom of a cookie sheet. (THE PARCHMENT PAPER WON"T BURN!)

5. Use semolina (or corn meal) over the oiled parchment or pan and top your pizza fresh out of the oven with freshly torn basil for those extra special pizza parlor flavor touches! 6. Par-bake extra pizza dough rounds after forming, cool and freeze in airtight plastic to have a start on your own pizza kit for later. Thaw, top, and bake as usual. Always use fresh quality ingredients for the best pizza!

Sir Lancelot flour is available through King Arthur Flour. http://www.kingarthurflour.com and I have seen Bounce or other "pizza flours" at Sam's Club and Costco, but in large bags only.

SALADS

For a simple Caprese salad, I alternate slices of fresh beefsteak tomato, fresh mozzarella, and basil leaves on a plate. Pour a tablespoon or two of really good olive oil across over the slices and enjoy. I usually grind some fresh black pepper and sea salt over mine and frequently add a few slices of fresh avocado and a splash of champagne vinegar, though a purist would not agree. If I am really hungry, I will cut the tomato and mozzarella into smaller pieces and use this over a basil and baby spinach salad and substitute a balsamic vinegar for the champagne vinegar. Both are excellent! Another option is to use your favorite pesto with a little extra olive oil or one of your vinegars, if needed, as your dressing.

I am also a big fan of Caesar salads and keep Romaine hearts around to chop up for a quick salad that I can add fresh Parmesan cheese and grilled and sliced chicken tenders when I prepare Nick's chicken wings or such. I found a wonderful prepared Caesar dressing from O Organics at Safeway (grocery store) that is outstanding! It is so easy and so convenient!

I have begun keeping a sweet basil plant that can be purchased at most grocery stores, for my Caprese salads. The salads are so fresh and wonderful and I use fresh basil in my Italian cooking, too, so the plant seldom has a chance to go to waste. The leaves add so much flavor to the salad and to pasta or pizza sauce that it is worth the average $2.99 I pay for each plant! A really tasty olive oil, a champagne vinegar, and a delightful blood orange balsamic vinegar that I found at a farmer's market up in the Northwest as well as fresh garlic, and a variety of peppercorns and sea salts help to round out my regular palette of salad and veggie taste treats.

With all of the varieties of kale and arugula and other tasty greens, salad never grows old! Add a handful of cheese (feta, bleu, etc.) crumbles, broken nuts (walnuts or pecans, candied or not) and fruit (sliced strawberries, craisins, pears, or blueberries, etc.) or throw on some leftover (or made just for) chicken or steak and top with a good olive oil and a splash of one of the many vinegars and you can have a complete meal!

QUINOA (KEEN-WHA) CHICKEN SALAD

½ C uncooked quinoa, rinsed (I like the Inca Red)
1 C water or chicken broth
1 C leftover cooked chicken, ½" dice
½ C white onion, finely chopped
¾ C celery, finely chopped
¼ C green bell pepper, finely chopped, optional*
2-3 T mayonnaise or Greek yogurt, just enough to moisten

Put rinsed quinoa and water or broth into a small pot with a lid. Bring to a boil, cover with lid and remove from heat. Set aside, covered, for 15 minutes. Fluff with fork, and place in a bowl to chill for 20 minutes. Gently stir in your cooked, diced chicken and chopped vegetables. Add mayonnaise or yogurt, and salt and pepper to taste, only if desired. Taste first! This is so good, as is, for a side salad, or in a pita with alfalfa sprouts, as a sandwich! Quinoa is an unusual and wonderful, nutty grain. I find myself making an extra chicken breast, when cooking, just to have it to make this salad! I love its crunchy goodness! I also like to double the amount of quinoa to have available. (Quinoa is a great side dish, too!) *If you are adventurous, leave out (or keep) the onion, and add green grapes, cut in half, and top with ¼ C blanched slivered almonds.

QUINOA SALAD

¾ C quinoa, thoroughly rinsed in a strainer, under cool running water (I prefer red or black quinoa, but regular quinoa is okay)
1½ C chicken broth (preferred, but water is okay)

Combine quinoa and chicken broth or water in a medium saucepan that has a tight fitting lid and bring up to a full rolling boil. Let boil for 2 - 3 minutes, then cover and reduce heat to a gentle simmer. Simmer for 5 minutes. Without removing lid, set off heat and let stand, covered, until cool. (Or use cooking method from previous recipe.) Fluff with a fork. (Makes 2½ - 3 C cooked.)

Dice into small cube:
2 medium carrots, peeled
1 medium-large green pepper, cored
1 medium-large red pepper, cored
3 - 4 celery stalks
1 medium red onion
1 – 1½ C frozen peas, unthawed

Combine diced vegetables with cooled and fluffed quinoa. Grind black pepper and sea salt over, to taste, and add your preferred choice of (gluten-free) Italian dressing, to moisten to your preference, or make your own vinaigrette or oil and vinegar dressing. Chill. This recipe can easily be halved. Enjoy within 3 – 4 days.

FARO AND QUINOA SALAD

¼ C faro (or wheat or spelt berries)
¼ C red quinoa
1½ C water (or chicken or vegetable broth)
½ of an English cucumber, quartered lengthwise and sliced
1 medium tomato, diced small
¼ C diced shallots (or red onion)
2 T balsamic vinegar
2 T freshly squeezed lemon juice (or cider vinegar)
Freshly ground sea salt and black pepper, to taste

Put grains into a fine mesh strainer and thoroughly rinse under running water to remove bitter coating on the quinoa. Drain and put into small, lidded pot, with water (or broth) and bring to a boil. Cover and continue boiling over medium heat for 5 minutes. Remove from heat and set aside, still covered, to cool. Place prepared vegetables in a medium bowl. Stir in balsamic vinegar and fresh lemon juice. Salt and pepper, to taste. Fluff grains with a fork (liquid should have been absorbed, if not, drain first) and stir into vegetables. Serve at room temperature or chill for later.

Note: You can use bottled Italian dressing or a balsamic vinaigrette to dress your salad, instead.

SWEET & SOUR ZUCCHINI SALAD FROM THE KITCHEN OF BLUE HERON CREAMERY COOK'S MOM

4 or 5 zucchini, green & yellow, sliced thinly

1/3 C chopped celery

1/3 C green or red pepper, chopped

1 T minced onion

Dressing:

¼ C honey

½ tsp salt

1 T dried dill weed

2/3 C cider vinegar

2 T vegetable oil

½ C sugar

Stir together dressing ingredients and pour over vegetables. Gently mix, then cover and let rest in refrigerator for one hour for flavors to combine. Submitted by Cleo Collette.

SWEET AND SOUR FRESH CUCUMBER SALAD

2 large cucumbers, peeled, halved lengthwise, and sliced thinly

1 small red onion peeled, halved and sliced thinly

½ tsp dried red chili flakes

½ C sugar

½ C water

5 T white vinegar

½ tsp salt

Place the cucumber, onion and chili flakes in a mixing bowl. In a small saucepan, over low heat, dissolve the sugar in the water. Remove from heat and stir in the vinegar and salt. Pour over vegetables in the bowl, stir, cover, and refrigerate until served. Yum! Freshly made, this can be refrigerated in jars for a week-no longer. This recipe makes 6 to 8 servings. Submitted by Cleo Collette.

THREE BEAN SALAD

1 - 13 oz. can cut yellow wax beans
¾ C sugar
1 - 13 oz. can cut green beans
2/3 C white vinegar
1 - 13 oz. can kidney beans
1/3 C olive oil, no substitutions
½ C chopped green pepper
1 tsp. pepper
1 medium chopped onion
1 tsp. salt

Drain the 3 cans of beans and combine. Add pepper and onion. Combine sugar, vinegar, and oil. Pour over vegetables and sprinkle with salt and pepper. Chill overnight. Toss to cover beans with marinade. Drain and serve. Serves 6-8. Submitted by Ginny Soucy-Beck

COLESLAW SALAD (CHEATERS WAY)

1 package shredded coleslaw
2 apples, cored and chopped
1 small can crushed pineapple, drained
½ - 1 C raisins

Mix together and add bottled coleslaw dressing. Submitted by Marilyn Bintz.

ORANGE TAPIOCA SALAD

1- 3 oz. pkg. orange gelatin*
1- 3 oz. pkg. instant vanilla pudding mix*
1- 3 oz. pkg. instant tapioca pudding mix*
1- 15.5 oz. can crushed pineapple
2- 11 oz. cans mandarin oranges, drained
1 - 8 oz. carton whipped topping, thawed
3 C water

In a large saucepan, bring 3 cups of water to a boil. Whisk in gelatin and pudding mixes. Return to a boil, stirring constantly. Boil for 2 minutes, then take off heat and cool completely. Fold in whipped topping, then stir in the fruits. Spoon into serving dish, cover and chill for at least 2 hours. *Sugar-free gelatin and pudding mixes are okay to use. Submitted by Fran Rothdiener.

BLACK-EYED PEA SALAD

1 can black-eyed peas, drained and rinsed
1 can white corn, drained
3 large tomatoes, diced just before serving
¼ C chopped cilantro
1 bunch green onion, cleaned and sliced
2 avocados, diced just before serving
½ C diced green pepper
Freshly ground black pepper & salt, to taste
For dressing:
¼ C red wine vinegar
¼ C olive oil
1 T minced garlic
1 tsp roasted or regular ground cumin (or to taste)

Mix dressing ingredients and pour over combined salad ingredients just before serving.

PASTA FRUIT SALAD

½ lb. corkscrew pasta
1 C cantaloupe or honeydew, cut into cubes
1 8 oz. can pineapple chunks, drained - reserve 2 T juice
1 C seedless green or red grapes
¼ C honey
¼ C sour cream
1 - 8 oz. carton low fat peach yoghurt
1 C fresh strawberries, hulled and halved

Cook pasta according to directions. Drain, cool, and place in a large bowl. Add pineapple, melon, and grapes. Combine reserved 2 T pineapple juice, honey, yoghurt, and sour cream. Toss with pasta mixture. Top with strawberries and serve. For a prettier presentation, line individual serving plates with leaf lettuce, then top with salad. Great for potlucks. Submitted by Pat Dunkel.

FRUIT SALAD DRESSING

1 C mayonnaise
¼ C pineapple juice
1 C sour cream
1/3 C grenadine
2 T powdered sugar
1 T lemon juice
2 T honey (citrus honey if you have it)

Whisk all together and chill. Serve with or over fresh fruit. This pretty pink dressing really compliments many combinations of fruit and makes a great dipping sauce, too!

FUMI SALAD

2 packages Ramen noodles (save flavor packet for another use)
4 T each, slivered almonds and sesame seeds, toasted quickly in a hot dry skillet over medium heat, just until golden brown, then cooled
1 green onion, thinly sliced
1 bag of coleslaw mix
Dressing:
4 T sugar
6 T rice vinegar
1 tsp salt
1 tsp freshly ground black pepper
1 C vegetable oil
1 tsp Accent, optional

Stir together broken Ramen noodles, almonds, sesame seeds, green onions, and slaw mix in large bowl. Combine dressing ingredients in small bowl and mix well. Pour over slaw mix and stir together before serving. Submitted by Brenda Speidel.

SLAW WITH RAMEN NOODLES

1 C sliced almonds
6 - 8 green onions, thinly sliced
4 tsp sesame seeds
1 16-oz. pkg. slaw
2 pkg. Ramen noodles, uncooked, chicken flavored
Dressing:
2/3 C vegetable oil
6 tsp white vinegar
dry chicken flavor packet from noodles

Break up dry noodles. Mix with slaw, green onions, almonds, and sesame seeds. Stir together the dressing ingredients and add to slaw mixture. Toss well and refrigerate for a couple of hours before serving. Submitted by Donna Clark.

MAIN DISH (7 LAYER) SALAD

Layer in order:

1 bunch of fresh spinach, well rinsed and drained, stems removed
5 – 6 C torn regular head lettuce or romaine lettuce
2 – 10 oz. packages frozen peas, rinsed and drained
4 hard boiled eggs, peeled and shredded
1 bunch green onions, cleaned and sliced
8 slices crisply cooked bacon, crumbled
1 - 8 oz. package Monterey jack cheese, shredded, reserve ½ C for topping
Frost with the following well combined mixture:
1 package dry Hidden Valley Ranch Dressing mix
½ C mayonnaise
½ C salad dressing
¼ C milk

Top with reserved cheese. Toss just before serving. This is a very pretty, even elegant presentation, when prepared in a large glass serving or punch bowl.

CAPRESE SALAD ON BABY SPINACH

3 C loosely packed baby spinach leaves
12 fresh basil leaves, sliced into strips
1 C grape or cherry tomatoes, halved
1 – 7oz. package bocconcini (fresh mozzarella balls, in water) drained and halved
3 T balsamic vinegar, or more, to taste
2 T olive oil, optional
Freshly ground black pepper, to taste
Freshly ground sea salt, to taste

Place rinsed and dried baby spinach leaves in bowl. Cut fresh basil leaves into narrow strips (stack leaves neatly, roll up from long side, and slice across roll into strips) and scatter over spinach. Top with halved cheese balls and tomatoes and sprinkle with balsamic vinegar. If using, sprinkle with olive oil, and grind pepper and salt over the salad, to taste. Serve immediately. You can use more basil leaves if desired, but I find them to be a very strong flavor and prefer to use lightly. I love the combination of basil with spinach. Champagne vinegar is also an excellent choice for this salad.

APPLE SNICKERS SALAD

1 – 3 oz. package instant vanilla pudding
½ C milk
1 – 8 oz. tub whipped topping
3 full sized Snickers candy bars, diced into ½" cubes
3 Granny Smith apples, unpeeled, cored and diced

Whisk milk into instant pudding until thickened. Stir in whipped topping just until smooth. Gently stir in apples and Snickers pieces and stir until combined. Keep chilled until just before serving. This is a great potluck item; otherwise I would eat it all in one sitting! Submitted by Joyce Keilman.

FROZEN SALAD

1 lg. box strawberry gelatin
2 C whipping cream
1 – 8 oz. package cream cheese, at room temperature
1 can crushed pineapple
1 small jar maraschino cherries, drained and halved
½ C celery, chopped finely
1 C mini marshmallows (or more, if desired)
½ - 1 C chopped walnuts or pecans

Make the gelatin as directed and chill until thickened, but not set. While the gelatin is chilling, whip the cream until thick and fluffy and blend in the cream cheese. Gently fold into the gelatin, along with the remaining ingredients, and pour into appropriately sized container or pan. Cover and freeze overnight. Set out for 10 minutes, then spoon out, or slice and place onto lettuce leaves. Submitted by Joyce Keilman.

SOUPS & STEWS

POT ROAST STEW

1½ - 2 lb. pot roast, cut in 1" cubes
½ C olive oil, plus additional, if needed for frying
1½ C flour
1 tsp salt,
1 tsp freshly cracked pepper
1 tsp crushed thyme
1 tsp marjoram
1 tsp savory
1 tsp garlic powder
1 tsp parsley
2 cans beef broth
1 can diced tomatoes, in juice
2 bay leaves
½ C raw pearled barley
3T Worcestershire sauce
2 large carrots, scrubbed and cut into ½" angle slices (or 1½ C baby carrots)
1 large onion, peeled and cut into large chunks
2 stalks celery, cleaned and cut into ½" slices
2 large russet potatoes, scrubbed, peels left on and cut into 1" cubes
1 C fresh or frozen green beans
1 C fresh or frozen peas

Mix together flour, herbs, salt, and pepper together in a large plastic bag. Drop meat cubes, a few at a time, into flour mixture and shake together well. Bring ½ C olive oil to high heat in a large, deep, heavy pot. Remove meat from bag, shaking off excess flour, and fry in small batches to a rich, dark brown. Add more oil as needed. Remove the meat to a plate (or your crockpot) to make room for more until all meat has been browned. Add in beef broth and tomatoes, lower heat to a simmer and stir up browned bits from pan. (At this point if you wish to use your crockpot, pour into crockpot, add in your meat and other ingredients and cook on low for 4 to 6 hours.) Add in meat, bay leaves, barley, Worcestershire sauce, carrots, onion, potatoes, celery, green beans, and peas. Let simmer for at least 1 hour or up to 3 hours to blend flavors. Taste and adjust seasonings and remove bay leaves to serve. This thickens as it simmers and is wonderful with fresh biscuits or rolls, and salad. This makes a lot but freezes and re-heats well.

COCK AND BULL

8 boneless chicken thighs
½ lb. beef round steak
1 medium onion
1 medium tomato (or small can tomato sauce)
2 medium potatoes
2 medium carrots
1 tsp. Worcestershire sauce
1 tsp. Italian herb seasoning
½ C beef broth
½ C chicken broth

Remove skin from thighs and trim fat. Cut steak into ½" cubes. Chop onions and tomato. Peel and cube potatoes and slice carrots. Place all ingredients into a crockpot and cook on low for 8 to 10 hours. Serves 4. Submitted by Bonnie Bellomo.

BROCCOLI CHEDDAR SOUP

1 bunch broccoli
¾ C celery, thinly sliced
1 medium white onion, chopped
2 cloves garlic, minced
1 - 5 oz. can evaporated milk
1 – 14 oz. can chicken (or vegetable) broth
4 T butter
4 T flour
¾ C shredded cheddar cheese
Freshly ground black pepper and salt, to taste

Rinse broccoli and cut into bite size pieces. Place into a 3 qt. saucepan with 1 C of broth.

Bring to a rolling boil, cover pot, and reduce heat and steam for 1 or 2 minutes. Remove from heat and take off lid. Set aside 1½ C of florets. In separate skillet sauté celery, onions, and garlic in butter until crisp/tender. Stir in flour and cook for two or three minutes, and while continuing to stir, carefully pour in evaporated milk. Cook until it begins to thicken, and then pour in remainder of broth, continuing to stir until blended. Add thickened mixture to pot of broccoli and simmer gently for 5 minutes until broccoli is done. At this point, if a creamy soup is desired, carefully use an immersion blender to bring to desired consistency. Add reserved florets and shredded cheese, cover pot, and remove from heat. Let set until cheese has melted, then stir and serve.

CREAMED BROCCOLI SOUP

1 large bunch broccoli
1 medium white onion, chopped
½ C baby carrots, diced
¾ C chopped celery, including some leaves
3 large cloves garlic, minced
2 C chicken broth, plus more, if needed
2 T butter
1 T olive oil
½ tsp freshly ground sea salt
1 – 3 oz. pkg. cream cheese, cubed ½"
½ - 1 tsp freshly ground black pepper
½ C freshly grated Parmesan, Asiago, or Romano cheese
1 T Tamari (natural soy) sauce

Clean broccoli and break into florets. Trim stems and cut into bite size pieces. Steam florets in ½-1 C of the broth until barely tender and set aside. Sauté stems, onions, carrots, celery, and garlic in butter and oil until onions are just beginning to brown. Add remaining chicken broth and simmer for 20 minutes, until very tender. Add cubed cream cheese and grate your choice of hard cheese over top of soup. Stir until cheeses are melted, then use an immersion blender to cream soup, if desired. Stir steamed florets and their broth into soup and warm for 3 – 5 minutes more. Do not boil.

MUSHROOM SOUP

8 oz. pkg. sliced mushrooms
½ C red onion, thinly sliced and halved
3 large cloves garlic, thinly sliced
3 T butter
2 T cooking sherry
2 C chicken broth
½ tsp freshly ground black pepper
½ tsp freshly ground sea salt
2 T flour
½ tsp dried thyme leaves
1 T Tamari (natural soy) sauce

Melt butter in large saucepan. Stir in onion and garlic and sauté over medium heat until just starting to brown. Add sliced mushrooms and cook until they have released their juices. Sprinkle flour over vegetables and cook and stir for 2 or 3 minutes, then add chicken broth, Tamari, sherry, and thyme. Simmer for 10 minutes or so to blend flavors, then serve. Quick and so easy!

ROASTED BUTTERNUT AND ACORN SQUASH SOUP

1 butternut squash, peeled, seeded, and cut into chunks
1 acorn squash, peeled, seeded, and cut into chunks
1 zucchini squash, sliced lengthwise, then again into ½" slices
1 large white onion, diced into large pieces
5 cloves garlic, sliced thinly
2 T olive oil, plus more for roasting squash
2 T butter
1 T smoked paprika
1 - 32 oz. box chicken broth or vegetable broth
1 T Tamari (soy) sauce
1 tsp dried basil leaf
¼ C sliced celery
1 medium white onion, chopped
½ tsp celery seed
½ to 1 tsp ground Spice Hunter Fiery Chile Fusion (or ¼-½ tsp ground white pepper)
½ C heavy cream
Freshly ground black pepper and sea salt, to taste

Very carefully, peel and seed butternut and acorn squash. Cut into chunks and put them on a baking sheet lined with parchment paper or foil (for easy cleanup). Drizzle with olive oil and sprinkle with smoked paprika. Roast the squash at 375° until tender and browning, about an hour. While the squash is baking, gently sauté onion, celery, and garlic in a large pot with 2 tablespoons of olive oil and butter, over medium high heat. When fragrant and just starting to brown, stir in zucchini. Stir broth into the pot, add roasted squash, basil and celery seed and turn heat down to a moderate simmer. Season with Tamari, salt and pepper, to taste, and simmer until vegetables are tender and flavors have had time to come together, at least 20 minutes. Taste, and adjust spices, if necessary, and add cream. Remove from heat. The soup can be served this way, or you can use your immersion blender to blend smooth. Serve with a dollop of sour cream for a pretty presentation.

POTATO LEEK SOUP

1½ lb. Yukon potatoes, peeled and diced
2 medium leeks, sliced in half lengthwise, thoroughly rinsed, and sliced again into ½" slices
2 T olive oil
2 medium carrots, diced small
2 medium stalks celery, diced small
2 cloves garlic, minced
1 - 32 oz. box chicken or vegetable broth
1 C packed, fresh baby spinach
1 C light cream
½ tsp each freshly ground black pepper and sea salt
¼ tsp white pepper

In a large stockpot, sauté carrots, celery, and garlic in olive oil for 3 to 5 minutes. Add potatoes, leeks, and broth to stockpot and bring to a boil, then reduce heat and add seasonings. Simmer for 10 – 15 minutes until vegetables are tender. Stir in cream and spinach and heat through. Do not boil.

PRONTO TACO SOUP

1 lb. ground beef
1 C uncooked spiral pasta
2 garlic cloves, minced
2 tsp chili powder (optional)
2 -14.5 oz. cans beef broth
1 tsp dried parsley flakes
1½ C picante sauce
1 – 14.5 oz. can diced tomatoes OR diced tomatoes with green peppers &
onions
1 C shredded cheddar cheese
tortilla chips

In a large saucepan, cook beef and garlic until meat is no longer pink. Drain.
Add the broth, tomatoes, salsa, pasta, chili powder and parsley. Bring to
a boil, stirring occasionally. Reduce heat, cover, and simmer for 10 – 15
minutes until pasta is tender. Top your bowl with shredded cheddar and
tortilla chips. Serve with salad and corn bread muffins. Submitted by Pat
Dunkel and her daughter, Carrie Francis.

SPICY CHICKEN RICE SOUP

2 - 14.5 oz. cans chicken broth
3 C cooked rice
2 C diced, cooked chicken
1 – 15.25 oz. can corn, undrained
1 C salsa
1 – 4 oz. can diced green chilies, drained
½ C chopped green onions
2 T minced fresh cilantro
½ C shredded Monterey jack cheese, for garnish

Combine all ingredients, except cheese. Bring to a boil, then lower heat and
simmer together for 15 to 20 minutes. Sprinkle cheese over top to serve.

BLACK BEAN SOUP

1 lb. black (turtle) beans, sorted and rinsed, then soaked overnight in covered pot
5 cloves garlic, minced
4 slices bacon, cut in half
1 medium onion, chopped
½ green pepper, chopped
2 – 15 oz. cans chicken broth
¼ - ½ tsp chipotle chili powder
1 tsp salt
2 tsp dried cilantro leaves
3 T lime juice
½ tsp cumin

Drain rinsed beans and place in large stockpot. Add chicken broth and enough water to cover the beans by 1 inch. Put bacon slice halves in pot and bring to a boil. Reduce heat to a simmer and cook, stirring occasionally, for 1½ to 2 hours, adding water, if necessary, until beans are tender. Add remaining ingredients and cook for at least 30 minutes longer or until beans are done to your liking and vegetables are tender. Remove bacon slices, if desired, and adjust salt, if needed. Mash some of the beans with a fork against the side of the pot to thicken if you prefer a thicker soup. Serve with a dollop of sour cream and some diced jalapeños or a tablespoon or two of fresh Pico de Gallo for an extra kick. I serve this alongside smoked baby back ribs for a wonderful side dish, and add any leftover pork to beans for a second go around. Yum!

SPICY TORTILLA SOUP

1 small onion, finely chopped
4 cloves garlic, minced
8 C chicken broth
2 cans Ro-tel brand diced tomato and chilies
4 T fresh cilantro, chopped
¾ tsp ground cumin
1 tsp sugar
Juice of 2 limes
2 C cubed cooked chicken
2 cans red or black beans, drained
salt & pepper, to taste
crushed tortilla chips
Monterey jack cheese, shredded

In a 6 qt. saucepan, combine onion, garlic, and broth. Bring to a boil, reduce heat and simmer for 10 minutes. Add all remaining ingredients except for crushed chips and cheese. Stir mixture and simmer for about 30 minutes to blend flavors. To serve, put hot soup in individual bowls and top with a heaping tablespoon of cheese and a handful of crushed chips over each. Garnish with fresh cilantro leaves. This is enough to serve 8 but can be divided. Submitted by Dort Halsted.

CHICKEN TORTILLA SOUP

1 package chicken breasts, bone in, with skin (approximately 1½ - 2 lb.)
1 - 32 oz. box chicken broth
1 medium white onion, diced large
3 - 5 cloves garlic, chopped or minced
1 - 4 oz. can diced green chilies
1 (or more, to taste) jalapeño, diced very small
¼ - ½ C freshly chopped cilantro
1 C frozen or fresh corn, or white hominy, optional
1 zucchini, unpeeled, in ½" dice, optional
Juice of 1 (or 2) limes
1 tsp ground cumin
Freshly ground sea salt & black pepper, to taste
1 tsp dried oregano
2 T olive oil
1 – 14.5 oz. can diced tomatoes, in juice
6 corn tortillas, cut into strips, and baked or fried until crisp (can use tortilla chips)
1 avocado, peeled, seeded and cubed
2 C shredded cheddar

Pour broth into a large pot and add chicken breasts. Bring to a boil, then reduce heat to a simmer and cook for 20 – 25 minutes, adding more water, if needed, until chicken is cooked through. Remove breasts from broth and let cool enough to handle. Remove and discard skin and bones, cut chicken into bite-sized pieces, and set aside. If desired, strain, chill, and de-fat broth. In a medium skillet, heat olive oil and cook onions until just tender, then stir in garlic and diced jalapeño. Remove from heat and add to broth. Stir in cumin, oregano, canned chilies and tomatoes with juice, corn or hominy, and zucchini, if used, then salt and pepper, to taste. Simmer broth for10 minutes, then add chicken and stir in lime juice and cilantro. Simmer for 10 minutes more. Place a small amount of cubed avocado and tortilla strips in each bowl and ladle soup over, then top with shredded cheese. Serve with warmed flour tortillas. (You can adjust this soup for heat, and optional vegetables, to taste, as desired.)

EVERYDAY CHILI

1 large white onion, chopped
1/3 C green pepper, chopped
1 C chopped celery, including some leaves
3 large cloves garlic, chopped
2 T butter
1 T olive oil
1 lb. lean ground beef
2 bay leaves
1 T unsweetened cocoa powder
3 T chili powder
½ tsp ground cumin
salt and pepper, to taste
1- 7¾ oz. can tomato sauce or El Pato Mexican tomato sauce (very spicy)
1 – 15 oz. can tomato puree or crushed tomatoes in puree
1-2 T corn meal, to thicken

Sauté all of the vegetables together in the butter and olive oil until tender. Crumble in the ground beef and cook and stir until no longer pink. Add tomato sauce and tomato puree and stir in chili powder and cocoa. Season with salt and pepper and add cumin and bay leaves. Let simmer for at least 30 minutes to blend flavors. About 10 minutes before serving, stir in 1 T corn meal. Let thicken and if needed, stir in remaining corn meal and continue cooking for at least another 10 minutes. Remove bay leaves. Top with grated cheddar and chopped onions and serve with crackers. This is good, made in the crockpot, and can also be used to make a taco salad

CHILL OUT CHILI

1½ lb. pork, cut into ½ inch pieces
2 C coarsely chopped onion
2 cloves garlic, minced
1 T vegetable oil
1 T chili powder
1½ tsp ground cumin
½ tsp oregano
½ teaspoon salt
1¾ C salsa
1 can (15 oz.) small kidney beans, rinsed & drained
1 can (15 oz.) black beans, rinsed & drained
1 pkg. (10 oz.) frozen whole kernel corn, thawed

Cook meat, onion, and garlic in oil, in a large saucepan or Dutch oven, stirring frequently, just until meat loses its pink color, about 8 to 10 minutes. Sprinkle chili powder, cumin, oregano and salt over meat; mix well to coat evenly. Add remaining ingredients. Mix well. Bring up to a boil. Reduce heat, cover and simmer 20 minutes, or until meat and vegetables are tender, stirring occasionally. Ladle into bowls; top with sour cream and minced green onions. Submitted by Cleo Collette.

KANSAS CHILI

1 - 2 lb. ground beef
3 T New Mexico chili powder
3 T whole-wheat flour
½ tsp oregano
¼ tsp garlic powder
¼ tsp black pepper
¼ tsp cumin powder
1- 8oz can tomato sauce
1- can Ro-tel
1- can beef stock
1- can chili beans or any red bean
Fry the meat until brown and crumbly, drain and add all the dry ingredients. Let rest for about 15 min, then add the liquids and simmer for 45 minutes to 1 hour. I sometimes mix ground beef and sausage, and add ¼ tsp of jalapeno powder if I want it a little warmer. Submitted by Don & Sharon Sells.

CINCINNATI STYLE CHILI

1-quart cold water
2 lbs. ground beef
2 C crushed tomato
2 yellow onions, diced
4 garlic cloves, minced
1T Worcestershire sauce
1 T unsweetened cocoa powder
¼ C chili powder
1 tsp cayenne
1 tsp ground cumin
2 T cider vinegar
1 bay leaf
¼ tsp ground cloves
1 tsp cinnamon
1½ tsp salt
Add beef and water to a 4-quart pot. Bring to a simmer while stirring until the ground beef is in very small pieces. Simmer for 30 minutes and add all of the rest of the ingredients. Simmer on low, uncovered, for 3 hours. Add water as needed if the chili becomes too thick. Refrigerate the chili

overnight to meld the flavors and the next day, remove the layer of fat from top before reheating and serving. To serve, spoon over cooked spaghetti and top with chopped onions and shredded cheddar and pass the oyster crackers.

CHILI RICE VERDE

4 C cooked rice
¼ C sour cream
1 - 4 oz. can diced green chilies
8 oz. jack cheese, shredded
salt & pepper, to taste

Mix all ingredients together. Pour into a 9X13" baking pan sprayed with non-stick spray. Bake at 350° for 35 – 45 minutes until hot and bubbly. Great for potlucks. Submitted by Pat Dunkel.

VEGETABLES & SIDES

MARINATED VEGETABLES

1 head cauliflower, broken into florets
1 bunch broccoli, broken into florets
1 red onion, cut in half, and sliced very thinly
1 small jar pimentos
Dressing:
1 C mayonnaise
½ C vegetable oil
½ C sugar
1/3 C vinegar
1 tsp dry mustard powder
Salt & pepper, to taste

Whisk dressing ingredients together and stir into prepared vegetables. Cover and chill for several hours, or overnight, to marinate. For a special treat, top with ¼ C crumbled cooked bacon and ½ C shredded cheddar cheese just before serving. Submitted by Jan Tamporello.

GRILLED VEGETABLES

Did you know that vegetables are wonderful when grilled? For most, it is a very simple preparation, just clean and slice, then spray very lightly with olive oil and grill until tender and flavorful. Times will vary, depending on the veggie and your personal preference. For eggplant, cut off the stem end and slice into ½" slices. Lay out on a cookie sheet and brush or spray both sides with olive oil. Lightly salt, if desired, before grilling. Zucchini, both the regular and the Mexican gray, can be quartered the long way, no need to peel, and also lightly brushed with olive oil and grilled. Asparagus just needs have the tough ends broken off. Onions and tomatoes can be cut into halves, oiling the cut edges and grilling. Peppers, green, red, orange, or yellow all give a wonderful taste treat when quartered and grilled. Corn on the cob can be prepared by first soaking, then pulling back the husk and removing the silk, before rinsing clean. Fold the husk back up around the corn and cook, letting it steam in its own husk. It can also be completely husked, then oiled and grilled. Smaller squash, like acorn, can be cut in half through the stem, and seeds removed. Oil the cut edge. Patty pan squash just needs to be cleaned and cooked whole. If you fear dropping smaller pieces into the fire, use a wire basket or tray made for grilling and sprayed with non stick spray (off the fire!), or substitute aluminum foil, sprayed and laid over the grill rack, poking a few holes through with your grilling tongs for extra flavor. Cook over medium high heat to perfection. Most take less time than your meats, but can cook alongside and then be kept warm over the cooler part of the grill, or returned to the grill later to re-warm before serving. Try it, you'll like it. Flavored salts and butter can season your vegetables, but go easy and let the natural flavors shine through. You can also roast your vegetables in a regular or convection oven on a parchment lined baking sheet, lightly drizzled with olive oil, separately or in any combination you prefer, for 45 minutes or until done to your liking, at 400^0 to 450^0.

STEAMED FRESH BABY SPINACH

1 T extra virgin olive oil
2 cloves garlic, minced
½ tsp freshly ground sea salt
1 - 6 oz. bag of baby spinach
Sauté garlic in olive oil, in a heavy saucepan (with a tight fitting lid,) over medium heat, just until translucent. Reduce heat and add rinsed baby spinach,

barely drained. Sprinkle salt over and place lid on top. After 10 minutes, gently stir. Spinach should be wilted and have just enough moisture to be steamed to your liking. Continue cooking if desired to the tenderness you prefer. Add butter or a squeeze of fresh lemon juice or champagne vinegar to serve, if desired.

STIR-FRY GREEN BEANS
½ - ¾ lb. fresh green or string beans
1 clove garlic, minced
2 T olive oil
½ tsp freshly ground sea salt
½ tsp freshly ground black pepper
1 T fresh lemon juice or soy sauce
Clean beans, break off ends and discard. If desired, break into smaller pieces. Heat a skillet to medium heat and add olive oil. Quickly stir in rinsed green beans and cook, stirring once or twice, for 2 – 3 minutes. Add minced garlic, salt and pepper and continue cooking just until crisp tender. Stir in your choice of lemon juice or soy sauce and serve. For a special touch, top with a sprinkle of sesame seeds. Asparagus can also be prepared this way with delicious results.

FRESH STEAMED ASPARAGUS

½ lb. fresh asparagus, rinsed well

freshly ground sea salt, to taste

2 T butter

water

Holding a stalk of asparagus near the top in one hand, gently grasp the cut end in the other hand and bend the two ends together. The asparagus will break where the bottom becomes woody. Continue with remaining stalks. If you do not have a steamer tray, place the discard ends in the bottom of a lidded saucepan or skillet and use them as a steamer rack. Place the rest of the asparagus over the discard ends and add enough water to just barely cover discard ends. Add salt, to taste, and bring water to a boil. Cover with lid, reduce heat, and steam to desired doneness. I prefer crisp tender, lightly buttered and salted and usually just steam my asparagus in my favorite covered saucepan, with a small amount of salted water without bothering with a rack. It takes just minutes and I can add the butter to the pot, gently shake and place directly on my plate. This is enough for 2 nice servings.

SUMMER SQUASH WITH ONIONS

2 medium fresh yellow summer squash

1 medium white onion, thinly sliced

Non-stick spray

 2 - 3 T butter

freshly ground sea salt, to taste

freshly ground black pepper

Gently wash squash and trim stem end. Slice into 1/8" coins, cutting fat end in half, if needed. Spray a large skillet with non-stick spray and heat to medium/high. Add butter and onions all at once and stir-fry for 1 - 2 minutes. Reduce heat to medium and add sliced squash. Gently stir in salt and pepper and cook for 2 - 3 minutes more until squash is barely tender. I prefer the flavor of white onions, but sweet yellow onions impart a nice flavor, also. This will serve 3 - 4 nicely.

SKILLET RED POTATOES

8 – 10 small red potatoes, scrubbed and cut in half or left whole if tiny
2 T olive oil
2 T butter
½ tsp freshly ground sea salt
1 tsp freshly ground black pepper
2 tsp dried parsley
½ tsp garlic powder

Heat a lidded skillet to medium/medium-high and add in oil and butter. Place potatoes, cut side down, into hot oil and cover. Cook for 3 to 5 minutes until browned on bottom. Stir gently, bringing browned sides to the top, cover and cook for 3 to 5 minutes more. Season with salt and pepper, parsley and garlic powder, and cook for 2 or 3 minutes more until tender. Remove lid, stir gently, and let potatoes crisp up, cooking uncovered, for additional 3 to 5 minutes. Serves 2.

EASY SCALLOPED POTATOES

1 - 28 oz. pkg. frozen O'Brien style potatoes
1 can cream of mushroom soup
1 can cream of celery soup
1 can spicy nacho cheese soup
1 - 12 oz. can evaporated milk

Defrost potatoes. Mix the three cans of undiluted soup and the milk together in a saucepan and heat to a simmer. Stir and pour over potatoes in a 9X13" baking pan. Bake in a pre-heated 350⁰ oven for 20 minutes, covered, then 50 minutes uncovered. Test potatoes in the center to be sure they are heated through. Submitted by Eileen Martin.

SCALLOPED POTATOES

4 medium russet potatoes, peeled and thinly sliced
½ C heavy cream
6 T butter, in small pats
1 C milk, more or less as needed
½ tsp cayenne pepper
½ tsp celery salt
¾ C shredded Parmesan
2 tsp freshly ground black pepper
2 T all purpose flour
½ tsp onion salt, optional
1 T dried parsley flakes

Spray a 9X9" baking pan with non-stick spray. Spread a layer of sliced potatoes to cover the bottom of pan. Pour cream over potatoes, add 2 T butter pats, and sift flour over all. Add another thin layer of potatoes, salts, ½ of the Parmesan, and pepper. Top with another layer of potatoes and pour over enough milk to just cover. Bake at 450⁰ for 45 minutes. Sprinkle remaining Parmesan over potatoes and continue baking for another 15 - 25 minutes, until thick and bubbly and lightly browned on top.

LEFTOVER MASHED POTATO BAKE

1½ - 2 C leftover mashed potatoes (however you make them)
2 egg yolks
1 tsp parsley flakes
2 T butter
1 tsp dry dill weed
2 T cracker crumbs
1 tsp dried chopped chives
salt, to taste
1 tsp onion powder
freshly ground black pepper, to taste
1 tsp garlic powder
1/3 C shredded Parmesan, Romano, and Asiago cheese blend (Kraft Natural Cheese)

Preheat oven to 375⁰. Place 2 T butter into an 8" square or round baking pan. Set pan in oven just long enough to melt butter. Remove from oven and swirl melted butter in pan just to coat. Set pan aside. In separate bowl, stir together potatoes, egg yolks, ½ of the shredded cheese, salt, pepper, and herbs. Pour extra butter from pan into potato mixture and stir to blend. Sprinkle ½ of crumbs over bottom of pan and mound potatoes into the pan. Do not smooth out. Sprinkle rest of crumbs and remaining cheese over top of mound and bake at 375^0 for 12 – 15 minutes or until golden brown and crisp.

POTATO PATTYCAKES

2 large russet potatoes, scrubbed and peeled, if desired
½ medium white onion
1 egg, lightly beaten
¼ C all-purpose flour
1/8 tsp baking powder
Freshly ground sea salt & black pepper, to taste
½ tsp smoked paprika, optional
Vegetable oil, for frying

Grate potatoes into a colander. Rinse under cold water until water runs clear, then squeeze and pat (nearly) dry and place in bowl. Grate onion into potatoes (or chop and add), then stir in egg, flour, baking powder, and seasonings. Heat about ¼" of oil in a large skillet over medium high heat until it shimmers. Without crowding, spoon 4 or 5 ¼ to ½ C portions of potato mixture into hot oil and cook, undisturbed, for 5 minutes. Carefully turn and lightly flatten slightly, and cook other side for 5 minutes more or until crispy brown. Serve hot, with a dollop of sour cream or ketchup.

POTATO PANCAKES

4 C shredded, peeled potatoes (about 4 large)
1 egg, lightly beaten
3 T flour
1 T grated onion
1 tsp salt
1 tsp pepper
Vegetable oil for frying (1/2" deep)
Rinse shredded potatoes in cold water and drain well. Pat dry with a couple of paper towels. Place in bowl and add egg, flour, onion, salt, and pepper. Mix well. Heat oil in skillet. Drop by 1/3 C into hot oil, flatten, and fry until golden brown. Turn and brown other side. Drain on paper towels.

POTATO PANCAKES (LATKES)

3 medium potatoes, peeled
½ small onion, grated
1 T all purpose flour
1 egg, beaten
½ - ¾ tsp salt
½ tsp freshly ground black pepper
1/8 tsp nutmeg (optional)
1 T chopped parsley
¼ C vegetable oil, for frying
applesauce or sliced peaches in syrup, optional, for serving
sour cream, optional, for serving
Coarsely grate potatoes and pat dry with paper towels. Put into medium bowl and add onion and egg. Stir and add salt, pepper, nutmeg, and parsley. Heat oil in skillet to medium-high and carefully drop in 3 - 4 large tablespoons full of potato mixture. Fry until crisply brown, then turn and repeat. I love these just lightly salted, but as a child we frequently ate these with canned peaches as a side, or even a main dish, and they were wonderful! Serves 3.

ZUCCHINI FOR ONE

Cleo Collette, my good friend and a subscriber from Oregon, has sent several ideas in for Miss Terry's Kitchen that are very worth sharing. This is an easy side if you have a toaster oven. Take one zucchini and wash and trim the ends. Make a little tray out of foil for your toaster oven tray and pour in about a tablespoon of olive oil. Cut the zucchini in four quarters the long way, roll each in the oil then shake them, one at a time in some Parmesan cheese. Bake (in the foil tray) at 400^0 until the cheese is browned and the zucchini is tender inside (13-18 minutes, depending on crispness desired).

ZUCCHINI CORN STIR FRY

1 or 2 ears of fresh corn, cut from cob** (or 1½ C frozen, defrosted, but fresh is better!)
1 medium/small green zucchini
1 medium/small golden zucchini
1 medium white onion, diced
3 cloves garlic, minced
¼ C chopped sweet red and/or green pepper
¾ - 1 C shredded cheddar cheese
2 T olive oil
1 T butter
salt and freshly ground black pepper, to taste
1/8 tsp white pepper, optional

In a medium non stick skillet, with a lid, gently steam cut fresh corn in 5 or 6 T water, covered, over medium heat until crisp tender (5-10 minutes). Drain. Add olive oil, butter, onions, peppers, and garlic to skillet. Sauté for 2 to 3 minutes. Cut ends off zucchini, cut in half lengthwise and then into ½" slices. Add to skillet. Gently stir, then cover and cook for 3 - 5 more minutes, just until squash is tender. If there is too much liquid, drain. Add salt and pepper and remove from heat. Sprinkle with cheddar cheese, replace lid for a minute for two for cheese to melt, then gently stir together and serve. **If you have a Bundt or angel cake pan, place end of corncob in center hole of pan, and when slicing the corn off the cob, all the corn (and mess) will fall right into the pan. I just slice bottom half of corn off the cob into pan, then turn end over end and slice off remaining half.

ZUCCHINI BLINIS (PANCAKES)

2 eggs
1 C grated zucchini
¼ C grated Parmesan
1 T minced red onion
½ tsp baking powder
¼ tsp freshly ground black pepper
¼ tsp garlic powder
¼ C flour
½ tsp salt
2 T olive oil for frying

Whisk eggs well. Add baking powder, baking soda, salt, pepper, and garlic powder and mix. Stir in flour and Parmesan and mix just until combined. Stir in grated zucchini and minced onion. Drop by heaping tablespoon into hot, lightly oiled skillet and fry until golden brown on both sides, re-oil skillet as needed. Serve with sour cream. This is a very nice side dish to accompany your meat for dinner or to enjoy as a snack.

ZUCCHINI CAKES

2½ C shredded zucchini
1 egg, beaten
2 T butter, melted
1 C breadcrumbs
¼ C minced onion
1 tsp Old Bay seasoning
½ C flour, for dredging
olive oil for frying

In a large bowl, combine zucchini, egg, and butter. Stir in breadcrumbs, onion and seasoning. Mix well. Shape into patties and dredge in flour. Heat oil to medium high heat in a heavy skillet and fry patties to a golden brown on both sides. This is a great side dish.

FRENCH FRIED ONIONS

1 C sifted flour
¼ tsp salt
1 egg, beaten until thick and lemon colored
¾ C milk
3 large sweet onions, unpeeled
vegetable oil for frying

Mix together beaten egg and milk. Stir in sifted flour and salt and beat until smooth. In a large kettle, heat 3" vegetable oil over medium heat until oil shimmers, approximately 375^0. Slice onions into 1/4" thick slices. Remove peel and separate into rings. Dip a few onion rings at a time into batter, making sure that each ring is completely covered. Using a large fork, lift one ring at a time into hot oil. Add in several more rings, without crowding. Cook, turning as needed, until golden brown on both sides. Drain on paper towels. Salt lightly as each batch comes out of the hot oil. Repeat with remaining onion rings until all are cooked.

EGGPLANT PARMESAN

1 - 1½ lb. eggplant, peeled and sliced ¼" thick
¾ C Parmesan cheese, divided
2 C (8 oz.) mozzarella cheese, shredded, divided
1½ C spaghetti sauce, divided
2 eggs, beaten
1½ C seasoned breadcrumbs
½ C flour
¼ C olive oil

Dip sliced eggplant into flour, then into beaten egg, then into herbed breadcrumbs. Heat olive oil in skillet and lightly fry eggplant slices until golden brown. In a 2-quart dish sprayed with non-stick spray, layer ½ of the eggplant slices, then ½ of the Parmesan cheese, ¾ C mozzarella, and ½ of the spaghetti sauce. Repeat layers, reserving ¾ C mozzarella. Bake at 350° for 35 minutes. Top with remaining mozzarella and bake for additional 5 minutes.

COPPER PENNY CARROTS

2 lbs. carrots, cleaned and sliced into 1/8" "coins", cooked until just tender, then drained and chilled
1 small green pepper, diced
1 medium onion, chopped
Dressing:
1 can condensed tomato soup mix
1 tsp prepared mustard
¾ C sugar (can substitute Splenda)
¾ C cider vinegar
1 T Worcestershire Sauce
Mix together dressing ingredients and stir into chilled carrots. Add onion and pepper. Combine well and chill overnight to combine flavors. Submitted by Marilyn Bintz.

GARLIC SPINACH

1 large bunch or small bag of fresh baby spinach, rinsed thoroughly
2 - 3 cloves garlic, thinly sliced
1 T olive oil
2 T fresh lemon juice
1 T butter
Heat olive oil in a skillet over medium heat. Stir in garlic just until aromatic, 1 – 2 minutes, then stir in spinach. Cover and cook, stirring occasionally, for 3-5 minutes, just until steamed and tender. Stir in butter and add fresh lemon juice. Salt, to taste, if desired. Serve immediately. Serves 2 - 3.

COTTAGE CHEESE AND BROCCOLI BAKE

1 - 16 oz. container cottage cheese
1 - 10 oz. package frozen chopped broccoli, thawed
¾ C shredded cheddar or Colby/jack cheese
3 T freshly grated Parmesan cheese
1 small jar roasted red peppers, drained and chopped
4 large eggs, beaten
1/3 C crushed croutons
Combine all ingredients except croutons and mix well. Pour into a 9" baking dish sprayed with non-stick spray and top with crushed croutons. Bake at

350⁰ for 45 minutes or until center is set. Let stand for 5 minutes before serving.

EASY STEAMED JASMINE RICE

1 C raw Jasmine long grain rice
2 C less 2 T water
2 tsp sugar
1 T rice vinegar (or cider vinegar)
1 T sesame oil (or vegetable oil)
½ tsp salt

Rinse the rice in a large wire mesh strainer until water is no longer cloudy. Put rice in a heavy 1-quart saucepan that has a tight fitting lid. Add the water, sugar, vinegar, oil, and salt and place over medium high heat. Bring to a full rolling boil, uncovered. Stir once, with a fork, reduce heat to a simmer, cover with lid and cook for 10 minutes. Remove from heat, but do not remove lid. Let sit for at least 5 minutes or up to 20 minutes, covered, then fluff with a fork and serve.

TOASTY OATSY TOPPING

2 C quick style oats
1/3 C Olive oil or 1 stick butter, melted
1/3 C grated Parmesan or Romano Cheese
1/3 C wheat germ
¼ tsp garlic salt
1 tsp Italian seasoning

Mix all ingredients well in a shallow, microwavable dish and cook on high, stirring each minute for five minutes or until mixture is golden brown. Cool, seal in a plastic bag, and keep in the refrigerator. Sprinkle this versatile topping on steamed vegetables or crisp salads. Toss the topping with hot pasta and diced, fresh Roma tomatoes and pass the grated cheese. Sprinkle it on crescent roll dough, then roll and bake. Or flatten refrigerator biscuits, top each with a teaspoon of topping, and fold, seal, and bake. Submitted by Fred Hammer

About The Author

Terry Russell is a full-time RVer and for the last fifteen years, her popular Miss Terry's Kitchen recipe column in the *Gypsy Journal RV Travel Newspaper* has delighted her many fans from coast to coast. When she is not cooking, or writing about cooking, you can find Terry paddling her kayak, spinning, weaving, crocheting, or just enjoying all of the wonderful adventures waiting to be found over the next hill and around the next bend in the road.

15579631R00134

Made in the USA
Middletown, DE
14 November 2014